Cambridge Elements

Elements in Historical Theory and Practice
edited by
Daniel Woolf
Queen's University, Ontario

PLURAL PASTS

Historiography between Events and Structures

Arthur Alfaix Assis
University of Brasilia

T0334086

CAMBRIDGE
UNIVERSITY PRESS

Shaftesbury Road, Cambridge CB2 8EA, United Kingdom

One Liberty Plaza, 20th Floor, New York, NY 10006, USA

477 Williamstown Road, Port Melbourne, VIC 3207, Australia

314–321, 3rd Floor, Plot 3, Splendor Forum, Jasola District Centre, New Delhi – 110025, India

103 Penang Road, #05–06/07, Visioncrest Commercial, Singapore 238467

Cambridge University Press is part of Cambridge University Press & Assessment, a department of the University of Cambridge.

We share the University's mission to contribute to society through the pursuit of education, learning and research at the highest international levels of excellence.

www.cambridge.org
Information on this title: www.cambridge.org/9781009462525

DOI: 10.1017/9781009036337

First published 2023

A catalogue record for this publication is available from the British Library

ISBN 978-1-009-46252-5 Hardback
ISBN 978-1-009-00516-6 Paperback
ISSN 2634-8616 (online)
ISSN 2634-8608 (print)

Plural Pasts

Historiography between Events and Structures

Elements in Historical Theory and Practice

DOI: 10.1017/9781009036337
First published online: November 2023

Arthur Alfaix Assis
University of Brasilia

Author for correspondence: Arthur Alfaix Assis, arthurassis@unb.br

Abstract: What is history about? This Element shows that answers centred on the keyword 'past events' are incomplete, even if they are not simply wrong. Interweaving theoretical and historical perspectives, it provides an abstract overview of the thematic plurality that characterizes contemporary academic historiography. The reflection on different sorts of pasts that can be the focus in historical research and writing encompasses events as well as non-events, especially recursive social structures and cultural webs. Some consequences of such plurality for discussions concerning historical methodology, explanation, exemplification, and representation are also outlined. The basic message, reinforced throughout, is that the great relevance of non-event-centred approaches should prompt us to talk more about 'histories' in the plural and less about 'history' in the singular.

Keywords: historical methods, historicity, history of events, social history, cultural history

ISBNs: 9781009462525 (HB), 9781009005166 (PB), 9781009036337 (OC)
ISSNs: 2634-8616 (online), 2634-8608 (print)

Contents

Introduction

History as a form of knowledge has long been regarded as a more homogeneous business than it actually is. We hear, think, and speak too much of history in the singular and too little of histories in the plural. This has continued long after the modern belief in history as a unidirectional, teleological, totalizing process was called into question. It keeps going, even when the sponsorship of cultural diversity and non-essentialized identities is embraced as a key function of historical knowledge. And it has also survived the erosion of an overarching notion of historical method, which by the late nineteenth and early twentieth centuries functioned as the cornerstone of the unity and distinctiveness of historical research. In connection with political, social, and cultural changes, waves of epistemic innovation have since originated some dissimilar, often clashing approaches to the past within academic historiography. Yet key consequences of such plurality have not been fully assimilated into theoretical debates on historiography and historicity.

Concepts in analytical frameworks will always be invested with a high degree of generality – ultimately, the latter is an essential aspect of what makes them concepts. It would hence be foolish to demonize sweeping notions such as 'the past', 'the historian', 'historical explanation', or 'historiography', and it is easy to notice that I myself cannot do without them. But general terms such as these can also be adjusted to better respond to the real diversity of ways of researching and writing history. What follows is, in this sense, more an attempt to fine-tune than to undo some basic ideas underpinning our understanding of historical thinking.

One of the most enduring and effective abstractions about historiography has been the assumption that the pasts addressed by historians amount essentially to unique events that either happened to people unwillingly or were enacted by them through individual action. This is a widespread assumption, shared not only outside the academic world, but also by many historians and philosophers of history. 'History is an account of events: all else flows from that', Paul Veyne once said,[1] elaborating on a very old opinion disseminated by Aristotle that still echoes in different contemporary metahistorical traditions and lines of thought. History as knowledge of particulars, as an idiographic science, as an essentially narrative mode of discourse or cognition, as a cultural mechanism for dealing with contingency – all these and other proposals tend to take *events* to be a key notion that encapsulates the empirical side of historical knowledge: an abstract summary of what it is that historians write histories about.

---

[1] Veyne, *Writing History*, 4.

Such views, I claim, are not sufficiently congruent with what history writing turned out to be in the intellectual worlds within which we have been living for quite some time. For it is easy to see that the historiographical landscape is marked by more than histories of events. Whereas historians, in general, still tend to take events much more seriously than the average social scientist, some consequential controversies surrounding historical research in the twentieth century spun around the quest for subjects and objects permeated by different temporalities and locatable below or beyond the metaphorical surface where events are assumed to take place. Among such elements, there are, for instance, institutions, ideas, environmental and material conditions, and symbolic patterns, all of which cannot be addressed in terms of simple sums of particular, ephemeral events – and whose geneses and transformations cannot be conceived in the same way as the particular changes that lower-scale events bring about.

In analytical or self-reflective assessments of historians' practice, it is therefore fitting to avoid looking upon the infinity of contents that we can take as constitutive of historical reality as if they all could be subsumed under a singular logic. From a metaphysical point of view, the pasts that historians address can be very heterogeneous. To be sure, many of the issues historians may choose to thematize easily qualify as events, but others do not. Historians' disagreements regarding methodological procedures and explanatory resources can often be traced back to differences over the kind of subject matter that is privileged in historical research. A brief glance at such disputes can show that while the *event* is an essential metahistorical category, it does not stand for all kinds of content on which historians usually focus their inquiries. After all, to assume that historiography is fundamentally about events is to condemn social and cultural historians to something many of their predecessors perceived as a methodological prison: *histoire événementielle*. That in real life historians have frequently managed to escape this is perhaps the best reason to admit that the pasts addressable through historical interpretation are plural. This is a key condition that we need to pay more attention to in our attempts to understand what academic historians do when they research and write.

In the following I intend to offer an overview of the plurality of academic historiography, in which the significance of events as a category for historiographical analysis and self-reflection is reassessed and recalibrated (though definitely not denied). With reference to historians' key practices and self-representations, I will attempt to chart content-related asymmetries that have constituted the historiographical field in the last century or so. Section 1 establishes a minimal metaphysical framework for the analysis, presenting a taxonomy of content categories, which includes events while also extending beyond them. This will provide a shorthand illustration of the assertion that events enjoy no monopoly over historians' attentions. Taken together, Sections 2, 3, and 4 comprise an attempt to ground that assertion with the aid of historical reasoning, in other words, by drawing on condensed historical surveys of contemporary historiography. They delve into events, social structures, and symbolic webs (or cultures) respectively, those elements from the taxonomy that stand for the prototypical subjects of political, social, and cultural history. Section 5 then takes a more decidedly theoretical approach and explores some of the consequences that thinking through the heterogeneity of content types in historiography may entail on discussions concerning methodology, explanation, exemplification, and representation.

I will speak a little more about my own methodological and meta-theoretical grounds in Section 1 and later at the beginning of Section 5. For now, let me just note that this is a historically informed theoretical survey about what it is that historiography is about. Unlike a great deal of the literature I have read while developing it, it is not primarily a text on epistemology or methodology, even if it is not disconnected from these realms and intersects some important methodological and epistemological issues (especially in Section 5). It is also not a text in what is often derogatorily called 'speculative philosophy of history', although the central issues discussed in it would by no means be alien to a material historical theory. As it zeros in on what can be called historiography's contents, themes, subject matters, subjects, or objects, it would be admissible to claim for it a label like that of a 'metaphysics of historiography'. But neither is this Element sufficiently systematic, nor can it go deep enough into its topics, to justify such a philosophically solemn designation.

An important measure for preventing semantic confusion is to clarify the sense in which the word 'historiography' will be used, for this is a notoriously tricky concept. Literally meaning the writing of history, the term can also be used as a label for theoretical analyses of historical methods or, especially, for histories of historical writing.[2] When I speak of historiography, nonetheless, I am not aiming at these or other forms of second-order study of historians' thoughts and doings. I am closer to the more literal meaning of the term, while extending it somewhat to include not only written epistemic products but also research operations connected with them. This use of 'historiography' allows us to narrow the semantic range of 'history', and to reserve this concept mainly for references to what was or what happened in the past. In the ensuing conceptual

---

[2] See Woolf, *A Global History of History*, 4–7.

division of labour, the relationship between history and historiography is placed in parallel with that between nature and (natural) science.[3]

My focus on academic historiography is another scope-related choice that should be spelled out. We all live in historical cultures – cultures within which connections to the past not only subsist spontaneously but are also purposefully cultivated through countless memory practices. Academic historiography is one among such practices, one that can claim to be a particularly rationalized and institutionalized mode of dealing with collective experiences.[4] It should not, however, be understood as synonymous with the discipline of history, for it encompasses a number of traditions of inquiry that are not exclusive to history departments at universities, as well as scholars who may not identify themselves professionally as historians. As a field or aggregate of fields, historical theory often goes far beyond the analysis of scholarly based histories,[5] but this Element will not. At its core are metaphysical nuances, methodological self-understandings, and research practices that can optimally be traced in the works of academic historians.

1 A Minimal Metaphysics

What has just been outlined suggests that the types of content addressable in histories are many and that the relationship between historiography and events should therefore be theoretically rescaled. For many practicing historians, such propositions sound rather obvious, but they become less so when they refer to those various and influential philosophical analyses of historical knowledge that take for granted that historiography is fundamentally about past events. The very existence of such disparity is an indication of how estranged historical theory and history of historiography have remained from each other, and I do not think we should be satisfied with such a state of affairs. Keeping this in mind, I will often resort to explorations into the history of historical research and methodology, as well as to mini-analyses of texts by historians. These procedures confer on some of the sections that follow a strongly descriptive character, which in itself should not be a problem. But they can occasionally eclipse the overall message that the sections, taken together, are designed to convey. To make up for the shuttling back and forth between history and theory,

---

[3] See Tucker, *Our Knowledge of the Past*, 1–2. Tucker's basic definitions of history as 'past events' and historiography as 'representations of past events' are, however, at odds with the main message of this Element.

[4] Rüsen, *Rekonstruktion der Vergangenheit*, 9–15; Rüsen, *Historik*, 221–52; Kuukkanen, *Postnarrativist Philosophy of History*, 11–13, 137–47, 192–7.

[5] Ohara, *The Theory and Philosophy of History*, 1, 40–2.

I shall begin by laying down a set of minimal metaphysical or ontological coordinates, which can be taken as a guide to the evolving argument.

Ontology and history have a long track record of not getting along well with each other. As a branch of philosophy centred on the study of the nature of being, ontology can be easily pitted against 'history', no matter whether this term is understood as referring to the becoming of entities, the transience of all things, or modes of knowledge dedicated to the explanation or representation of change.[6] But historiography, and this is one of my main claims, is not only about events but also about 'non-events';[7] it is not only about becoming but also about *being*. It is therefore in no way absurd to ponder on the possibility of something like an ontology of historiography – for instance, in the sense of a discussion of the relevant entities usually referred to in historical interpretations.

Here, and further on, I follow that spirit but deviate somewhat from its letter. The term 'ontology' applies well to several of the content-related coordinates that are about to be mentioned, but not to all of them. Historiography – the statement must now be reversed – is not only about being but also about *becoming*. If we are to work out a minimal chart of what features thematically in histories, we have to make room not only for entities but also for events. 'Ontology', in that regard, may project an unhelpful emphasis. This is why I am resorting to the more generic and event-friendlier term 'metaphysics' and its derivatives to point to the field of phenomena usually foregrounded in histories, understood in a typological way.

It is important to underscore that this terminological option is not indicative of a speculative concern with history 'as a whole', comprehending not only the past but also the present and the future, no matter how much reflections of this sort are legitimate, and probably even necessary, for sustaining and renewing the cultural relevance of historical studies.[8] Also, it must be clear that I do not intend to develop a fully fledged theory of historical reality, but just a minimal set of categories drawn from the history of historical research and methodology, and then analytically polished and complemented to some extent. What I am trying to get at, hence, is no pure metaphysics, and not just because the subject matter is not primarily philosophy or because I am not a philosopher myself. In a sense, it is an impure one, for it projects metaphysical problematics onto a knowledge practice – that is, onto historiography – thus intermingling with questions more often deemed epistemological.

---

[6] An inspiring attempt at mediation is Ian Hacking's idea of a 'historical ontology', which he, drawing on Foucault, advances as a retrospective characterization of some of his own philosophical investigations. See Hacking, *Historical Ontology*, 1–26.

[7] Pomian, 'Evento', 218–19.

[8] Fillion, 'The Continuing Relevance of Speculative Philosophy of History'; Munz, *The Shapes of Time*, 7–9.

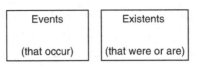

Figure 1 Events and existents

In the literature on history and historiography it is unusual to find discussions about the basic constituents of historical reality, let alone discussions of the kind that would take into account the diversity of contemporary historiographical practice. A rare and useful resource is a typology by Allan Megill, based precisely on the distinction between becoming and being. Accordingly, actions and sufferings *occur*, whereas characters and settings *exist*. Historical texts convey ever-different ways of seeing these four elements in interaction. Megill proposes that we treat actions (carried out by characters) and sufferings (impinged on them) as *events*, while reserving the term *existents* to designate both characters and settings.[9] What is appealing in this typology is that it gives us a basic metaphysical framework within which it becomes very clear that histories are not only about events unfolding in time, but also about entities exhibiting a temporal dynamic quite distinct from that characteristic of *événementiel* phenomena.[10] 'Existents' is an adequate tag for grouping them together, albeit one that is strange to historians' methodological language.[11]

It has sufficiently been said that historiography should not be conceived as being fundamentally about events. But now we can add that phenomena which cannot be conceived as events can be clustered as existents. This basic distinction is schematized in Figure 1.

To unfold the idea that histories are not only about events but also about existents, it is useful to weave these two categories into some synoptic insights drawn from the history of contemporary historiography. Political history is the

---

[9] Megill, *Historical Knowledge*, 95.

[10] For a similar framework, based on the distinction between events, lives, and societies as types of subject matter in historical descriptions and interpretations, see McCullagh, *The Truth of History*, 88–111. See also Little, *New Contributions*, 52–3 and Scholz, 'Philosophy of History', 248–51. I will often use the adjective '*événementiel*' in its original French form, as there is no good English equivalent to it. Anglicized alternatives such as 'evenemential', 'evental', or 'evential' sound too artificial and have not yet found their ways into standard dictionaries.

[11] It is, nonetheless, a term that has been used by ontologists for centuries as a generic designation for 'what exists'. In recent years, the word has been increasingly adopted by anthropologists, especially those inclined towards what is often called the 'ontological turn' in anthropology. But neither general ontologists nor ontologically oriented anthropologists tend to stress the existent–event distinction that is essential to my argument. Megill, whom I following here, borrowed it from Seymour Chatman's comprehensive theory of narrative. See Chatman, *Story and Discourse*.

first label that comes to mind when one speaks of histories centred on events, but it is easy to see that the latter concept also applies to domains outside the political. An earthquake, a marriage, a gang fight, the signing of a business contract, a technical invention, the conclusion of an artwork: all these and many more could be historical events, but their political meanings or impacts would not necessarily be what mattered most about them. Even so, in the history of twentieth-century historiography attempts to shift the focus of historical knowledge from the political doings of relatively small elites to new subjects tended to go hand in hand with a repudiation of event-centred epistemics.

I will defer a more detailed discussion on events for the moment, but it is important to anticipate that the word is used here as a blanket term covering *individual* actions, sufferings, thoughts, and processes, no matter whether they are intentional, or how intentional they can be shown to be.[12] It could also indicate *collective* actions, sufferings, and thoughts, of which I shall not speak much. In addition, the word 'events' encompasses larger-scale processes and slow-motioned social or cultural changes. This is a wide scope of application that a more throughgoing approach to the metaphysics of historical events would need to revise and rebuild. We will, nevertheless, remain close to the generic uses of historians, who tend to unproblematically mix events and actions, or attribute actor qualities to collective entities. In a sense, though, we will also follow the inflationary use of the term by most philosophers of history, for whom 'event' designates a variety of occurrences ranging from short-term individual actions to socially transformative processes of very large scale.

'Existents' encompasses an equally vast range of asymmetrical phe-nomena. Under this category we could first place the human *persons* who initiate, help shape, and experience events. They are the most obvious and concrete *characters* featuring in history texts, but they are not the only ones. *Social individuals* are sometimes equally, if not more, import-ant. Historians do speak of family relations, military units, corporations, political and juridical bodies such as assemblies and courts, as well as many other kinds of social groups, which are assumed to act, suffer, change, have some sort of consciousness and certainly individuality, even if they are collective phenomena very distinct from the individual per-sons constituting them.

---

[12] Megill does not mention thoughts and processes in his brief discussion of events. Furthermore, he uses 'happenings' instead of 'sufferings'. The use of the latter category was advocated by Rüsen, *Historik*, 32–49, 114–28.

Characters, especially human persons, are essential. Historiography is not only thematically related to them, but it is, of course, generated by and for human beings. This apparently trivial circumstance encapsulates much of the hermeneutical depth of historical knowledge. We will not, however, focus on this connection, just as we will also not be able to pay close attention to characters. Yet in addition to characters, Megill also includes *settings* in the list of historiographically relevant existents, and these will indeed be more extensively examined in the following pages. Borrowed from narratology, the settings metaphor may well cover various kinds of structures of repetition that frame or constrain individual actions, sufferings, and thoughts, and which resist downward reduction to the individualistic level.

We can now understand much of the appeal of the 'new histories' envisaged or brought into being in international waves since the early twentieth century as stemming from novel ways of addressing settings. While agreeing that a history devoid of events would barely be thinkable, several of the twentieth century's most innovative historians insisted on searching for deeper levels of historical reality below or beyond the eventful 'surface' with which earlier generations seemed to be content. In a given spatial-temporal configuration, they sensed, events are not only connected to contingencies and disruptions. From a certain distance, most of them could be perceived as markers of regularities and continuities, of general patterns somehow resembling what the sociologist Émile Durkheim conceived of as 'social facts'. Inspired by different branches of the social sciences, leading historians took such patterns as key historical themes and gave them great explanatory weight. Accordingly, they started to write histories focused on the social, economic, or geographic conditions under which characters acted and interacted in a given time and place. A good part of such conditions remains largely outside the scope of people's awareness. Histories that emphasize the framing of past social life by such consciousness-distant structures often introduced themselves or were introduced as social histories.

Although I concentrate on human-made *social structures*, one might note that less-human-related or non-human-related conditions, such as those directly linked to cosmological, physical, geological, chemical, biological, or geographical factors, can also be of great historiographical import – as several environmental, geo-historical, big-historical, or global-historical approaches nowadays attest. However, another type of setting can be prioritized in histories intending to go beyond events. Because they are general, durable, and entail repetitions, immaterial, *symbolic webs* should also be accounted as structural phenomena. Languages, myths, religions, the arts, the sciences, and all sorts of scholarly traditions rely on such semiotic structures, as well as everything pertaining to the realm of the social imaginary or of collective representations. The concept of culture works as a synthesis of the broad array of shared symbolic forms and goods that enable and constrain social experience in a certain time, place, or group. The boundaries between symbolic and non-symbolic structures are hard to fix, posing an open problem for social theorists. But historians often traced them in practice, for instance when they contrasted sub- and super-structural conditions, or when approaches oriented towards geography, demography, and econometrics were challenged in the context of the 'cultural turn'. In a rough synthesis, we can say that a distinctive mark of cultural webs is that they are proximate to subjective experience. Cultural historians specialize in studying this kind of subject matter, and a good part of their work could be described as that of decoding past practices and representations so as to shed light on patterns of meaning that gave cultures their main shapes.

These brief references to the history of historiography underscore the plausibility of differentiating between events and existents and of connecting both to some additional subtypes of historiographically relevant phenomena. The obtained set of metaphysical categories can be enlarged, problematized, and refined, but in the current form they already provide enough of a toolbox for us to map out abstractly what histories are about. The categories discussed, their rankings and interrelationships are brought together in Figure 2.

As indicated, the items and levels in this rudimentary taxonomy will not receive equal treatment in the following sections. We will only zoom in on events, social structures, and symbolic webs. The main reason for doing so is

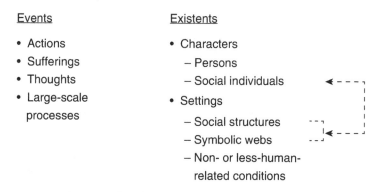

Figure 2 Historiography's basic content categories

that the set composed by the selected categories affords us a means to bridge historiography's metaphysics and history. Indeed, as already previewed, we can relate events, social structures, and symbolic networks in fairly straightforward ways to political history, social history, and cultural history, respectively; that is, to three major labels connectable to historians' methodological practices, self-perceptions, and debates. The selected categorial frame echoes, therefore, a usual distinction between alternative paradigms of historical research that have coexisted, sometimes peacefully, as complementary knowledge resources, but perhaps more often tensely as rivals in a historicity contest presumed to be a one-winner game.

The three methodological possibilities to be surveyed do not, by any means, represent all that can be done under the name of history; not even within the subdisciplines of political history, social history, or cultural history. Besides, the taxonomy composed to make sense of them could most certainly be either enlarged with new categories, or redesigned to accommodate important matters that do not fit well within it. Where do we draw the line between a sequence of individual actions and a long-term process? Can we put in the same bag events that are perceivable by contemporaries and 'invisible', long-term events that can only be conceptualized retrospectively by a later historian? Should we have had 'objects' or 'resources', 'meanings' or 'symbols' complementing the list of basic types of *existents*, alongside *characters* and *settings*? Where would be the proper place of ideas, and if they were to be classified as existents, how could the ensuing distinction between thoughts and ideas be tenable? What about those entities such as social classes or institutions that in some contexts can qualify as both characters and settings at the same time?[13] Can we speak of structures without raising questions as to their knowledgeability by actors who think symbolically? And if we cannot, how could symbolic webs, which indeed have an essentially structural character, be distinguished from other kinds of social structures?[14] Can the cultural be opposed to the social in such a way? Could it, moreover, be opposed to the natural? We will delve into some of these questions later on, but it is important to caution in advance that none of them can be satisfactorily settled here. This is no 'theory of everything', and we soon realize that the taxonomy just introduced not only casts a brighter light on some neglected issues, but also generates collateral problems it cannot fully solve.

---

[13] To allow for that possibility, Figure 2 includes a two-pronged line connecting 'social individuals' and 'settings'. See Section 3.2.

[14] In Figure 2, the rectangles representing 'social structures' and 'symbolic webs' are juxtaposed to indicate that tracing the borderline between them in an unambiguous way is no simple task. See Section 4.1.

Here, general metaphysics and social theory appear not as ends in themselves, but as means to some other end. We will approach general metaphysical or social-theoretical issues, but we will do so in the context of reflections rooted in the history of academic historiography, especially from the late nineteenth century onwards. As these reflections are meant to be dialogical, I seek to build upon the self-consciousness of practicing historians instead of parting ways with it. Such an approach resembles that of most phenomenologists and many anthropologists in that it takes seriously historians' native categories, that is, the forms and contents of their methodological consciousness. I reckon that while moving back and forth between history and theory of history in such a way we may be encouraged to think outside the box of event-centred assumptions that underpin many of the current views on history and historiography.

2 Events

2.1 A Foundational Notion

'Am Anfang war die Tat' ('in the beginning was the deed') – this is how Goethe allowed Faust to come to a solution to the translational puzzle posed by the first sentence in St John's Gospel. The proposition would apply, *mutatis mutandis*, to historiography. Here too, deeds, actions, or events are strongly tied to a foundational principle. Wherever it originated, history writing began as the history of events. When in Ancient Greece texts became known by the name of 'histories' they were centred on deeds, in cases such as Herodotus' or Thucydides', political and military actions that were not so far away from the present and parts of which they had themselves witnessed. For centuries after them, most histories produced in the West and also in other cultural spaces were by and large about events. Even today, many academic historians are mainly concerned with registering occurrences, getting them right, explaining how they came to pass. The large majority of history books, documentaries, and historical fiction that reaches out to larger audiences gravitate around historical events. Even in histories intent on questioning event-centric approaches, a good degree of attention to singular actions, sufferings, and thoughts is inescapable.

As an understandable consequence, the most common way of abstractly telling what histories are about has been by assuming that they are about events. In fact, for many historians, most historical theorists, and virtually everyone outside the academic world, the very essence of history as a form of knowledge lies in the task of piecing together a profusion of events into a truthful, evidence-responsive, sequential narrative. Thus constituted, history's factual narratives are seen as offering possibly true or at least plausible explanations of certain actions and changes deemed memorable for various reasons. Yet the existing body of reflections on events as a metahistorical category is meagre in comparison to the centrality assigned to them in the practice of historical studies. Scholars writing about historical events from philosophical or methodological viewpoints often observe that we encounter here a largely under-theorized notion.[15] Moreover, channels of communication between the literature on events produced respectively by reflective historians and historically minded philosophers have been, to date, quite narrow.

In a general sense, events can unfold before the eyes of the public or within the confines of the mind (as a thought or a decision), be distinguished into homogeneous activities or culminative performances, be fragmented into atomized units, or put together into temporally extended processes.[16] To see some unity in these diverse possibilities, one must contrast events with non-events; that is, with other basic metaphysical categories such as, among others, persons, other living beings, and physical objects. These three tend to be 'prime actors in events'.[17] They all are, to recall the notion introduced earlier, *existents* that can be said to be, whereas *events*, rather, happen.[18]

It goes without saying that the term 'event' is employed in contexts that go far beyond the theory and practice of historical knowledge. A collision of subatomic particles, a stellar explosion, the birth of a jaguar, a traffic accident – all these and many more can be categorized as events. Nevertheless, what matters most to us here is not the event as a general philosophical problem,[19] but the more particular idea of the *historical* event that is so central in perceptions and discussions of what historiography is about. Historical events happened to human persons or communities and were often products of actions. This is hardly controversial, but the waters become muddier as soon as we consider that the notion applies to occurrences that are, again, immensely diverse. In historians' and historical theorists' uses, 'events' can refer to individual or collective deeds and sufferings of many sorts, to individual thoughts, including those by people identifiable as intellectuals in a wide sense, as well as to longer term processes leading to social, cultural, or institutional change. Moreover, one should note that some events are indissociable from the subsequent impacts they had or continue to have. Others were attributed with distinctive, 'historic' meanings already by their contemporaries, or by later interpreters, whereas the vast majority of occurrences in past and present worlds were not and never will be. Groundbreaking events that triggered rapid changes in the lives of millions of people (such as the fall of the Berlin Wall or the Covid-19

---

[15] Bösch, 'Das historische Ereignis'; Jung & Karla, 'Times of the Event', 78; Sewell Jr, *Logics of History*, 225; Tamm, 'Introduction', 6.

[16] Casati & Varzi, 'Events'.   [17] Casati & Varzi, 'Events'.

[18] Romano, *Event and World*, 1–5.   [19] See Zeleňák, 'Two Approaches to Event Ontology'.

pandemic) of course differ from unexceptional, routine events (such as my going for a walk this morning) – not to mention complex eventful processes like climate change, whose effects come at a slower, though cumulative pace. These and other incongruences do not stop people from conceiving of an uncountable number of differentiable occurrences in terms of events.

I have no intention of fighting this firmly established conceptual state of affairs. By moving on without systematically regarding possible (and in many contexts crucial) distinctions such as those between events, actions, sufferings, and processes, and by using 'events' as a short word for both individual and collective experience, I remain close to the historians' 'native' categories in the hope that the benefits accruing from this will outweigh the logical costs incurred.

The semantic frame with which we are engaging is manifestly knotty, but we can refine our preliminary definitions in a further dimension, namely, the one which comprises criteria for deciding on the very historicity of events. Here, at least three basic meanings could be distinguished in historians' actual dealings with what happened or possible uses of the term 'events': (1) all that occurred as perceived by contemporaries; (2) dramatic or unexpected occurrences which are or turn out to be full of consequences, often featuring as reference points for profound temporal changes, crises, or collective traumas; (3) large-scale processes only addressable in hindsight by non-contemporaries.

Note that the historicity of events of type 1 is fully determined by their contemporaries, whereas that of type 3 is only ascertained by non-contemporaries. Unlike the former, the latter type comprises long-term changes that are not visible to the naked eye of contemporaries, but only to the abstract eye of posterior historians. Examples of these include, among others, changes and fluctuations regarding climate, the environment, demography, prices, or power relations.[20] Historical events of type 2, in turn, fall in between the other two, since they are perceived as significant by their contemporaries, and yet generate consequences that may extend far beyond the witnesses' lifespan – consequences which, therefore, are only addressable by later historians. Wars, revolutions, and ethnic cleansings are prototypical examples of events in this sense. Indeed, type 2 could actually be taken as a subtype of type 1, as the latter encompasses all that happened, provided that it was perceived and registered by a contemporary and that testimony or evidence regarding it is available to a later historian, irrespective of whether or not it turned out to be impactful in the longer term.

Histories of events are traditionally histories of surprise-triggering or changemaking occurrences that, as the saying goes, 'made history'. This means that they do not care much for the neutral, perhaps effectless events of the first type,

---

[20] These examples of long-term changes are borrowed from Pomian, 'Evento', 231.

nor for the abstract, 'invisible' events of the third type. William Sewell Jr, for instance, reserves 'historical events' for occurrences that were perceived as extraordinary by their contemporaries and that, in addition, subsequently resulted in 'durable transformation of structures', such as the arrival of James Cook in Hawaii in 1779, or the Storming of the Bastille ten years later.[21] In other words, Sewell identifies historical events with type 2 events. However, since we easily find in contemporary historiography a wealth of significant references to other types of events, we should avoid closing the historical realm too much or too soon. Historians have become increasingly resourceful in the cognitive use they give to occurrences that fit the first type but not the second. In addition, the ascent of different forms of structural historiography has given type 3 events ever greater prominence. Crucially, historians have developed sophisticated ways to relate events of different types to one another and to non-*événementiel*, structural configurations. They can, for instance, resort to occurrences exempt from markers of surprise or contingency as a means to illustrate the operations and mutations of large social or cultural settings.[22]

It is remarkable that, in each of the three connotations, events as addressed by historians contrast sharply with events that feature in the explanations of natural scientists. A crucial difference is that historical events are not standardizable. To attempt to establish fixed descriptions of past events that could be employed in all historical interpretations or explanations that feature them would be in vain. There is no unit beyond which an event would be indivisible, no permanent rule (and often also no logically compelling reason) for distinguishing between an event and a process.[23] In historiography, comments Paul Roth, 'events do not come prepackaged, like elements on some periodic table'.[24]

To ponder on what such circumstance entails, consider a set of interrelated occurrences like World War II (hereafter WWII), which one might place in the second of the three aforementioned types. In the framework of a big-historical interpretation, as in David Christian's *Maps of Time*, it may appear unproblematically as a single event – in fact, a rather secondary one, in comparison with epochal thresholds like the modern 'fossil fuel revolution' or the formation of the first stars of the universe some 13.5 billion years ago.[25] In books that centre on the twentieth century, on the other hand, WWII tends to be given much more attention, but this does not rule out the possibility of introducing it as a sort of sub-event in an even larger occurrence. Eric Hobsbawm, for instance, speaks of the 'thirty-one year war', thus evoking the long European

---

[21] Sewell, *Logics of History*, 228.   [22] See Section 5.3.
[23] Mink, *Historical Understanding*, 199–201; Little, *New Contributions*, 44–6.
[24] Roth, *The Philosophical Structure*, 13.   [25] Christian, *Maps of Time*.

war of the seventeenth century to compound the two world conflicts of the first half of the twentieth century.[26]

Taking yet another approach, we could start with WWII and then disaggregate the event into smaller military, political, or international criminal occurrence units. We could consider 'WWII' as a conceptual tool for putting together occurrences and experiences and for simplifying our linguistic reference to them, and then be tempted to think that the 'real' unit events were actually the many military battles and operations conducted from 1939 to 1945. But this would not make the hypothetical quest for a fixed rule from which to demarcate an event any easier. What we take as a battle is also an aggregate of smaller events that occurred in different moments and venues. The bombardment of Hamburg, for example, took place from late July to early August 1943. It can surely be broken into many sub-events, for instance, each of the more than 2,500 individual aerial missions it comprised. But such smaller occurrences, it turns out, also could be disaggregated into even smaller ones. Exercises in event subdivision can go on and on.[27]

The plasticity of events has always been there as a more or less recognized element in both the historiographical game and historicized life. In the nineteenth century, Johann Gustav Droysen pointed out that what we usually call a fact is often a retrospective abstraction. By this means, historians summarize a myriad of other sub-events, setting them together – since, for instance, they can be linked to a common purpose, cause, or effect. Arguing against the well-shared assumption that a rigorous comparative study of sources could always yield the 'objective fact' (*objektive Tatbestand*), Droysen stresses that a battle or an insurrection is not an event at all to those involved in its unfolding. What is 'objective and real' then are rather those 'thousands running to and fro, screaming and striking at each other'.[28] Historical occurrences, he was suggesting, do not have a fixed unity. No interesting history can come out when one is exclusively intent on disaggregating events and getting rid of the conceptual abstractions that surround them. This is not to say that events whose historiographical treatment demands very low levels of abstraction would not belong in histories. It is rather a statement on the import of events conceived in synthetic fashion, those that were not experienced as such by past actors and witnesses. Even a classical history of events, Droysen may remind us, used to go beyond a mere translation of contemporary actors' and observers' perceptions. Among the events it deals with, there are not only those perceived by contemporaries,

---

[26] Hobsbawm, *Age of Extremes*, 22, 52–4.   [27] Munz, *The Shapes of Time*, 26–34.
[28] Droysen, *Historik*, 95–8.

but also those synthesized by the historian on the basis of a critical examination of such perceptions.

A basic reason underlying the impracticability of standardized demarcations of historical events is that the significance of what happened is both disputed and subject to change. Historians cannot forbear assessing events in light of moral, political, religious, and epistemic values. They usually address pasts that are somehow significant for them and their audiences. Very few devote their time to studying either events or non-*événementiel* subjects and objects about which they are completely neutral. Of the many different subjective attitudes and inclinations that are found among historians, indifference vis-à-vis the studied pasts must be the rarest.

A temporal dynamic is added to all this when we note that as time goes by historians are given the opportunity to reassess and rescale past events on the basis of effects and information that only emerged afterwards; that is, effects and information that could not have been assimilated into the contemporaries' perspective. Moreover, temporal distance entails that posterior historians live in a social world marked by epistemic, moral, religious, and political values that may be substantially different from those of the past at issue. And, as new events continue to unfold, the interval between the original event and historians continues to expand. The event will be regarded in light of newer consequences, which may change the meaning it has for those addressing it. It may become more or less significative than it was to the contemporaries or to previous historians; in any case, it will hardly remain significative in the same way it was, previously or originally. (None of this presupposes that events only have one meaning at a given time: historians of the same generation, as well as witnesses and contemporaries, often arrive at very different, conflicting views of the same set of occurrences.)

When we say, then, that events are not standardizable, we mean among other things that they are aggregable and fractionable, that they can be scaled up and down in time and space.[29] This feature, in turn, is given wide support by the impossibility of stabilizing the significance of events once and for all. The temporal dynamics sketched here cannot but strongly affect the significance that the pasts have for historians or the meaning the latter attribute to the pasts. For all that, it is plausible to infer that the very meaning of events is to a large extent dependent on historians, their cognitive repertoires, extra-cognitive interests, temporal viewpoints, and social circumstances. However, it is definitively not entirely dependent on them. An obvious *condictio sine qua non* for

---

[29] On issues of scale in historiography, see Hughes-Warrington, *Big and Little Histories*; and Retz, *Progress and the Scale of History*.

event-centred historiography is the availability of evidence on events, and especially of testimonies. Events of types 1 and 2 are, in the words of Krzysztof Pomian, 'perceived changes', that is, discontinuities, emergences, rearrangements, and disappearances that a contemporary observer must have been able to see and register. This formulation implies that for linguistic records of change perceptions to be generated, more is needed than perceiving witnesses – contemporary human subjects able to see, listen, write, draw, or speak. Some sort of modification must have really taken place in the extra-subjective world if we are to speak plausibly of someone perceiving; otherwise, it would be better to refer to some other kind of mental act.[30]

The situation of historiography with regard to meaning is, therefore, quite complex. The mentioned records are not mute, meaningless traces on which later historians simply impose meanings. While historical interpretation generates new meanings for the present, it cannot fail to take into account earlier meanings and interpretations; it builds upon or against them, but never in a vacuum. Historians' interpretative performance, in other words, is not reducible to a present-oriented projection, for it is the fruit of an intertemporal negotiation. The emerging meaning is not unilaterally imposed, but dialectically constituted upon previous meaning layers.[31] What happens when meaning-constituting historians address significant past events could be labelled in Gadamerian terms as a fusion of temporally distinct, meaningful horizons.[32] As in historiography in general, histories of events can only be written amid a complex dialectic of subjective constructions and objective constraints.[33] To expand on this point would take us too far from our aims; suffice it to reiterate here that historical texts are neither to be compared to simple reconstructions or translations of past occurrences, nor to be seen as vectors of the unfettered imposition of meanings from the present on meaningless past experiences.

2.2 Explainable End Results and Memory Landmarks

Having briefly explored the nature of historical events and the temporally complex dynamics of their significance, we can now move to more specific methodological issues attached to the history of events. For this purpose, it will be useful to introduce the contrast between recollecting and explaining in the analysis of what is at stake when historians make sense of past occurrences. As with so many other cliché-conducive topics of Western culture, this distinction (and its application to the understanding of the doings of historians) leads us back to Aristotle.

---

[30] Pomian, 'Evento', 219–22.   [31] Ricœur, *Time and Narrative*, I, 72.
[32] Gadamer, *Gesammelte Werke*, I, 311–12.   [33] See Rüsen, *Historik*, 85–96, 103–7, 156–8.

'There are two classes of demonstrations, one giving the Fact, the other the Cause of the fact', whereas 'the highest science is that which gives both the fact and the cause.[34] In these two non-contiguous sentences from the *Posterior Analytics*, Aristotle introduced what we can call 'description' and 'explanation' as two main modes of understanding and established a hierarchical relationship between them. In the few (though posthumously influential) passages in which he came to speak about historiography, Aristotle made it clear that it was fated to comprise descriptive recollections but no explanations. History would be fit to present, for example, 'what Alcibiades did, or what he suffered', but it was poorly equipped to tell why he did what he did or why he suffered so.[35] Historians' unilateral attachment to particulars, to singular, unrepeatable events, would prevent them from arriving at causal demonstrations. Without these they would never be admittable in the club of the most honourable forms of knowledge.[36]

But when we think twice about what historians have actually done, we soon realize that they have scarcely followed Aristotle in the way they relate to the events that feature in their accounts of the past. Almost always, they have offered more than recollections or descriptions of unique occurrences deemed particularly significant. Histories of events have also encompassed proposals as to how we should see these events in terms of their causal connections.

The search for causes behind or beyond events has been an integral part of the historiographical agenda, at least since Polybius who wrote his extensive *Histories* in the mid-second century BC to make sense of what he viewed as an immensely significant event in his contemporary age, the ascent of Rome to the rank of world power. A crucial desideratum for him was to know 'by what means and under what system of polity the Romans in less than fifty-three years have succeeded in subjecting nearly the whole inhabited world to their sole government'.[37] To explain why such a unique achievement was possible, Polybius wrote a 'universal history' formatted on a very wide geographic scale, in which occurrences of many sorts are seen together as signs of (and simultaneously as steps towards) the materialization of a single *telos*.[38] The thesis that events from different times and places concurred with the common end of Rome's ascent to world power was instrumental for his attempts to do more than simply reminisce particulars. It gave him a main reference point for treating events as constituents in causal explanations that could claim some level of generality for themselves. In addition, in the course of his text he also

---

[34] Aristotle, *Posterior Analytics*, 33, 70; quoted by Kuukkanen, 'Fact'.
[35] Aristotle, *Poetics*, 12.　　[36] See Daston, 'Baconian Facts', 40–1.
[37] Polybius, *The Histories*, I, 2–5.　　[38] Balmaceda, 'La Antigüedad clásica', 36–7.

discussed issues of historical causality in a more reflective way, most especially while referring to the factors behind the occurrence of wars.[39]

A mode of knowledge centred on causal explanation can hence be made compatible with another focused on the recollection of past singular dealings. Histories of events tend to do both, in varying degrees, even when tensions between these two operations can easily appear – as can be seen, again, in Polybius' text.[40] In monographic studies focusing on a main event, explanatory components tend to be particularly undisguisable. A good example is Francisco Doratioto's *Damned War*, a well-researched account of what was arguably the major armed conflict involving independent South American states, the war between Paraguay and the Triple Alliance formed by Argentina, Brazil, and Uruguay (1864–70). This presents in detail a myriad of smaller-scale occurrences related to its main subject, thus standing for a classical history of events. But it is also charged with an explanatory goal that is addressed directly in the introduction, concluding remarks, and especially in the first chapter, which amounts to a history of Paraguayan foreign relations until fifty years before the military conflict began. Doratioto explains the causes of the war by contesting the influential view that British diplomacy manipulated Argentina and Brazil into taking military action against Paraguay. On this account, Paraguay would have been perceived as a transgressive antagonist by its neighbours and by Great Britain because it was emerging as a modern and economically independent state, supportive of an increasingly egalitarian society. Doratioto equals this view to a conspiracy theory. He claims that the war had nothing to do with British imperialism and that it was caused by more regional and contingent factors.[41]

Events under historical explanation need not be strictly military or political. In *The Dead Will Arise*, Jeff Peires brings to the fore the puzzling Xhosa cattle killing of 1856–7, an event of cataclysmic consequences, during which around 40,000 people died and after which British domination over the traditional territory of the Xhosa at the Eastern Frontier of the Cape Colony entered into a crucial new phase. Peires argues that a necessary cause of the cattle killing and the ensuing famine was the spread of bacterial lung disease among the cattle, originating in September 1853. But he shows that such an epidemiological development unfolded in a social environment already stressed by British interferences that had, in previous years, led to military defeats, material losses, populational displacements, threats to the chiefs' traditional sources of political authority, and transformations in the religious belief system.[42] It is only by

---

[39] Walbank, *Polybius*, 157–60.　[40] Ibid., 162–6.
[41] Doratioto, *Maldita Guerra*, 18–23, 88–96.
[42] Peires, *The Dead Will Arise*, 124, 138, 165–80.

considering these massive and disorienting changes, Peires suggests, that one can explain the popular echo of a millenarist prophecy that urged the Xhosa to slaughter their cattle and destroy their crops. Desperation induced by epidemics and favoured by colonial interferences made thousands of people prone to drastic sacrifices, without which, they came to believe, the impending resurrection of the dead and regeneration of the world would be held off.

Like so many historians, Peires and Doratioto take their respective focus events as outcomes, and then develop explanations as to how each came about, in which previous events and circumstances appear as links in causal chains. However, events do not need to be treated as consequences begging for causal explanations – and this may be another important effect of their plasticity. They can also feature in analyses centred on what 'happens' to them after they take place; on what Marek Tamm suitably calls the 'afterlife of events'.[43] Here events are not end results to be explained but rather starting points for memory processes shaped in response to the living circumstances of posterior individuals, groups, or generations. As mentioned, an event may over time gain multiple and conflicting layers of significance. These are constituted by different ways of remembering it that are often only loosely related to what actually happened, and which keep in direct connection with the uses and functions the event can play in political agendas and social discourses. The event's subsequent representations, uses, and functions can become subjects of historical interpretation no less than its antecedent causes. To give a methodological label to the latter alternative, Jan Assmann introduced the term *Gedächtnisgeschichte*, which can be translated as history of memory or mnemohistory. For him, in contrast to the traditional focus on the how and why of events, 'mnemohistory is concerned not with the past as such, but only with the past as it is remembered'.[44]

As a result, it is possible for historians to be only secondarily interested in the wealth of factual details surrounding the Xhosa cattle killing or the War of the Triple Alliance in South America, or in the causal chains that might explain them. Instead, historians can set out to investigate how these events were remembered afterwards, and how these memories themselves became factors in the political and social worlds from which they emerged. One could show, for instance, how British colonial officials in the second half of the nineteenth century effectively promoted a conspiratorial view of the Xhosa cattle killing that suited their imperialist purposes; or how, in the second half of the twentieth century, this view was rejected by anti-apartheid and Black Consciousness intellectuals, while the thesis that the killing was masterminded by the British

---

[43] Tamm, 'Introduction'. See also Dosse, 'Historical Event', 31; Jung & Karla, 'Times of the Event', 82.

[44] Assmann, *Moses the Egyptian*, 8–9.

governor of the Cape Colony gained ground.[45] Analogously, scholars of South American history may explore the ways in which the war against the Triple Alliance has up to the present constituted 'the essential basis of Paraguayan social identities',[46] or delve into the roles played by the event's memory in social narratives defending or criticizing regimes and institutions in the three countries of the winning side.

Mnemohistorical interpretation often touches on issues that are full of echoes in the present world that hosts it. Whenever this is the case, it intersects with hermeneutically inspired philosophical frameworks such as those synthesized in Gadamer's notion of *Wirkungsgeschichte* (history of effect) or in Derrida's hauntology.[47] Hermeneutical approaches to events can comprise the study of the original meaning horizons under which they take place or the subsequent waves of reception and appropriation that animate their afterlives. But a hermeneutics of events would only come full circle if it were also able to illuminate the ways in which part of what happened keeps connected to the meaning horizons hosting the interpretative enterprise itself. It could then show how interpreted pasts may haunt the present of their interpretation and unexpectedly pop up like ghosts, turning their absence into an uncomforting sort of presence.[48] And it certainly is to bring to mind how past events can still be effective in the present; how they keep affecting current people and their lifeworlds. This includes, of course, people committed to scholarly historical understanding, who may thus become better enlightened regarding the very conditions under which they act as knowers.[49] Philosophical-hermeneutical or deconstructivist heuristics can hence enrich histories that take events as starting points for memory processes (or as landmarks within living traditions), and so promote historians' self-reflectivity by furthering their awareness of historical understanding's own historicity.

Mnemohistorical strategies for dealing with events have been put into practice with high degrees of methodological self-awareness and increasing popularity in many disciplines – in history, since at least Georges Duby's *The Legend of Bouvines*, a 1973 work published in the framework of a traditional history of events book series, but which ended by focusing on changing memories of the 1214 battle up to the middle of the twentieth century.[50] A focus on subsequent impacts, appropriations, and resignifications of occurrences can illuminate the reasons why events came to be significant to us and others, revealing the path by which the social uses and functions of events were constructed, changed, or

---

[45] Offenburger, 'The Xhosa Cattle-Killing Movement'.

[46] Capedevila, *Paraguay bajo la sombra de sus guerras*, 18, 161–76.

[47] Tamm, 'Introduction', 4–5.   [48] Kleinberg, *Haunting History*.

[49] Gadamer, *Gesammelte Werke*, I, 304–12.   [50] Dosse, 'Historical Event', 39.

imploded. For all that, mnemohistorical approaches represent an outstanding expansion of our historical interests in general, as well as a major innovation within the specific domain of the history of events.

They can, furthermore, expose some clear insufficiencies in older approaches to events. There is no denying that all that happens has causes and hence – at least in principle and provided that we can access enough information – may be explained by reference to the factors we put together when we talk about a context. But, as Romano reminds us, events sometimes upend their causative antecedents, and when they do so they are to be understood 'less from the world that precedes them than from the posterity to which they give rise'.[51] The vast majority of events do not reveal such power, remaining as just 'innerworldly facts', in Romano's terminology. But those that do, that is, events that are somehow 'world-establishing', cannot be sufficiently understood simply in causal terms: again, they surely have causes, but these 'do not explain' them. In reference to this latter sort of event Romano states: 'Understanding events is always apprehending them on a horizon of meaning that they have opened themselves, in that they are strictly nonunderstandable in the light of their explanatory context'.[52] Romano is thinking of what – to mark his criticism of traditional concepts of 'subject' – he calls the 'advenant', human beings inasmuch as they are 'constitutively open to events'.[53] But no major modifications are needed for his anthropologically shaped reflections to apply also to historiography, that is, to a mode of knowledge frequently attracted to 'historical' events that claim to be understood not so much in terms of their anteriority as their posteriority; not only in light of their causative contexts, but also of their context-altering or world-making effects.[54]

None of this means that the old ways of doing history of events are simply to be abolished. Recollections and explanations of events, especially political events, provide informational databases that are essential to other historiographical approaches. In addition, histories of events feed epistemic interests that are legitimate in themselves and which will not vanish, even if most academic historians today find the limitation to the *événementiel* rather inacceptable.[55] Adapting a claim by Frank Ankersmit regarding political history, one could say that the history of events in the classical sense is 'the link between myth and legend on the one hand and all of historical writing on the other . . . [It] is prototypical of all history. There is something inevitable and supremely self-evident about [it].'[56]

Thus, both the older causal concerns and the newer orientation towards events' effects play important epistemic roles. In the plural constellation of

---

[51] Romano, *Event and World*, 38.   [52] Ibid., 41, 152.   [53] Ibid., 20, 49.

[54] Jay, 'Historical Explanation and the Event', 563–8, adapts Romano's phenomenology of events to expose the limits of contextualism in historiography, especially in intellectual history.

[55] Pomian, *Sur l'histoire*, 387–92.   [56] Ankersmit, *Meaning, Truth, and Reference*, 250.

contemporary historical cultures, there is plenty of room for both lines of inquiry, and historians have been finding creative ways to hybridize them, often with great success. Moreover, beyond all their methodological differences, the two share a similar trait. When all is said and done, the older and the newer histories of events tend to be attracted to the same kind of foundational, surprise-triggering, or disruptive events (represented by the second type in the list introduced in this section).[57] They have both paid little attention to the more ordinary events that are rather context-reinforcing than epoch-making; that happen to or are set in motion by many, often nameless individuals instead of a few, eminent ones (i.e. to events of the first type). In fact, for the last century or so, concern with ordinary events and ordinary people went hand in hand with attempts to extend the focus of historical interpretation towards themes that do not fit in the flexible suit of the event. These attempts often postulated that historical reality is multi-tiered, and that events are located only in the more visible of those tiers. To move beyond the histories of events, one had to take inspiration from neighbouring social sciences and venture into deeper layers of reality. In other words, one had to shift the historiographical focus from the *événementiel* on to the structural. In the following section, we will explore some essential aspects involved in this shift.

3 Social Structures

3.1 On the Genealogy of Structural Histories

Since when have historians been attentive to non-events? This is a thorny question, not least because searches for absolute origins, including those pertaining to historiography, are usually unavailing. Nonetheless, it is reasonable to say that structural views were already implicit in the founding documents of Western historiography. In their texts, authors such as Herodotus, Thucydides, Polybius, and Tacitus proceed on the assumption of a fixed human nature and presuppose that change only occurs according to patterns and cycles that apply to different cases. Without (tacit or explicit) reference to generalities like these, they would have no means to scale how unique were their focus events, not to mention causally explaining them.[58] This condition applies not only to history writing's ancient classics, but probably also to all kinds of texts about past events. Even an un-narrativized chronicle of seemingly random events selects occurrences according to implicit criteria that must be endowed with some degree of generality if they are to determine what can and cannot count as noteworthy. It is, in sum, hard to imagine what a history of events totally

---

[57] Karla, 'Controversial Chronologies', 137.   [58] Koselleck, *Zeitschichten*, 44–7.

disconnected from general assumptions concerning human experience, patterns of change, or relevance criteria would look like.[59]

Structural phenomena were always implied in histories of events, but equally crucial is that for a long time they remained under-processed in the methodological consciousness of historians. Ibn Khaldûn deserves to be mentioned as one of the earliest scholars to have developed a perspective that was methodologically aware, designed to track history's internal causes beyond the external surface of contingent events. He envisioned a new form of historiography featuring both singular events and social habits of a general nature; a 'new science' manifestly endowed with the kind of philosophical dignity Aristotle had denied to older histories.[60] Ibn Khaldûn's methodological reflections would remain unmatched in their depth and range, at least until the elaboration of another very impressive proposal for a 'new science' of human issues by Giambattista Vico, more than 300 years later.

Only after Vico would similar structural approaches to historical interpretation gain ground. As noted by Mark Phillips, a very significant 'enlargement of the boundaries of the historical' was consolidated in the eighteenth century, as philosophers and historians insistently looked in different directions beyond political action, to include common-sense beliefs, science, commerce, manners, sentiments, or aesthetic experience as subjects of historical interpretation.[61] Holistic concepts like 'age', 'civilization', 'zeitgeist', 'spirit of nations', or 'universal history' were then articulated to signal unity beyond divergent forms and levels of experience. They were neither anti-political nor incompatible with eventful histories, but they placed political events within larger explanatory frameworks, the conception of which demanded not only historiographical but also philosophical (as well as artistic) skills. Not coincidentally, this project was often labelled 'philosophical history', and among its practitioners we could count many of the most famous thinkers of the Enlightenment age. To facilitate the conceptualization of long-term developments or comparisons between temporally or spatially distant social orders, eighteenth-century historical authors even experimented with non-narrative modes of presentation as in the Scottish 'conjectural histories' or in the synchronic tables with which German historians attempted to give a visual expression to their philosophically enhanced sense of historical totality.[62]

---

[59] Pomian, 'Evento', 226–7.

[60] Mahdi, *Ibn Khaldûn's Philosophy of History*, 70–1, 152–3, 181–3.

[61] Phillips, *Society and Sentiment*, 14–20.

[62] Araújo, 'Imagens da simultaneidade'; Cheng, *Historiography*, 29–60; Phillips, *Society and Sentiment*, 171–89; Woolf, *A Global History of History*, 293–313, 332–40.

That concerns with refining non-event-centric forms of historiography persisted throughout the nineteenth century is often overlooked. In countless texts of the period, one comes across the antithesis between a mere history of events and a history that reaches out to invisible facts or non-events, whereby the methodological superiority of the latter is constantly acknowledged.[63] Wilhelm von Humboldt, for instance, admitted that the 'historian's task is to present what actually happened', stressing however that an event (*das Geschehene*) 'is only partially visible in the world of the senses; the rest has to be added by intuition, inference, and guesswork'. Only in this way could one perceive the 'inner causal nexus' connecting occurrences synchronically and diachronically.[64] That nexus is a function of Humboldt's idealistic notion of ideas, which postulates the existence of a deeper, non-immediately visible, and causally crucial level of historical reality. Similar routes from particular occurrences into more general, deeper, and non-observable layers of historical reality were traced later by theoretically minded historians like Alexis de Tocqueville, Droysen, or Jacob Burckhardt.

Dissatisfactions with event-centric historiography were expressed by many nineteenth-century historians, and alternatives to it were put in place, for instance, by liberal-minded scholars attracted to the historical trajectory of collective entities like the middle classes. François Guizot even came to see in the struggles between the bourgeoisie and the nobility the driving force of long-term social transformations. 'Modern Europe', he stated, 'was born out the conflict between society's different classes'.[65] In 1843, in the context of an institutional analysis, Alexandre Herculano suggested that history should be something more serious than 'the exclusive narration of two marriages, four funerals, and six battles'.[66] Very far from the anecdotal intent ridiculed here were many of the histories focused on economic, institutional, legal, and also cultural subjects written in the nineteenth century. Innumerable examples could be sought, especially if we bear in mind the big picture comprising all the humanistic disciplines and fields, which by then were predominantly infused with historical theories and methods.

Let us briefly focus on the two authors from the long-nineteenth century who exerted the biggest influences over later structural approaches to history: Marx and Durkheim. The kind of historical materialism advanced by Marx entailed that ideas, cultural processes, and political activities and fluctuations could not be sufficiently understood unless their roots in the material configurations of a society were spotlighted. 'Economic structure' was for him 'the real foundation,

---

[63] Pomian, 'Evento', 215.   [64] Humboldt, 'On the Historians' Task', 57–8.
[65] Quoted in Prost, *Douze leçons*, ch. X.   [66] Herculano, *Opúsculos*, VI, 260.

on which arises a legal and political superstructure and to which correspond definite forms of social consciousness'.[67] Such structures constituted by all the relations between individuals and the 'material forces of production' in a given society have, for Marx, the status of facts. But they are abstract facts that contrast with the singular events usually at the centre of traditional political histories.

The same can be said of Durkheim and the chief methodological notion associated with his name, that of 'social facts'. There are, as he determinedly insisted, facts that do not fit into the category of events, and which are also not primarily physical, organic, or psychological in nature: 'they consist of manners of acting, thinking, and feeling external to the individual, which are invested with a coercive power by virtue of which they exercise control over him'.[68] Individuals live under collectively shared circumstances that they can neither control nor freely change, and which can be said to condition, constrain, limit, or even cause their doings and sufferings. Scholars of the human world will be stuck with a low-grade mode of knowledge so long as they undervalue the study of such invisible social phenomena. This was the already-old insight that Durkheim radicalized and turned into the cornerstone of a science of society, and which was more estranged from historical perspectives than never before. Even so, it would exert a great influence over the historiographical scene, especially in France.

Several other 'founding fathers' of the modern social sciences – such as Georg Simmel, Max Weber, Talcott Parsons, and Claude Lévi-Strauss – also provided powerful impulses for the study of social frameworks that comprised and constrained past events and actions. To this we should add the intellectual influence exerted by Sigmund Freud and later by the whole structuralist movement. From all these sources came models of analysis and conceptual tools which, once appropriated and adapted, helped establish new approaches to historiography throughout the first half of the twentieth century.[69]

The preceding genealogical remarks illustrate how complements, alternatives, or contestations to the event-centric views of the past may have been almost as old as historiography itself.[70] Non-*événementiel* approaches, however, only rose to a position of methodological pre-eminence during the course of the twentieth century. In France, François Simiand acted as a key mediator who helped spread sociological concepts and concerns among the community of historians. In a now classical text from 1903, he criticized the over-concentration on political facts as an 'idol of the historical tribe'. Historians would only get rid of it, he implied, if they learned to prioritize the repetitions

---

[67] Marx, *A Contribution to the Critique of Political Economy*, 20–1.
[68] Durkheim, *The Rules of Sociological Method*, 21.   [69] Malerba, *Ensaios*, 88–100.
[70] See Ankersmit, *Meaning, Truth, and Reference*, 246–49.

and regularities underscoring a 'positive science' of the social domain, instead of the unique, contingent events that used to attract their attention.[71]

This message either echoed or had parallels in many works of history produced at the time in several different places. Simiand's critique expressed a leitmotif of what – in an analogy with established periodization practices in literary history – we could call a 'modernist moment' in historiography. This conceivable period, which extends from the last two decades of the 1800s to the mid-twentieth century, can be linked to the achievements of a good number of innovative authors from different national contexts, and not limited to those of Western Europe and North America.[72] Talk of a 'modernist moment', nevertheless, should not trick us into supposing that a sudden and all-embracing paradigm shift then took place. In fact, methodically innovative historians like Karl Lamprecht, Johan Huizinga, Lucien Febvre, and many others were all trying to reach beyond events, but this impetus often pushed them in quite dissimilar directions. Besides, despite their differences they formed a kind of vanguard that, while commanding increasing recognition, for a long time remained a minority in the general context of historiographical production. Everywhere, most academic histories written in the period certainly remained non-'modernist' in terms of style, choice of subject, and method.[73]

Even so, by the mid-twentieth century, the sense that events are at best secondary to historical understanding was widespread among historians who were then becoming respected authorities within their intellectual fields. Fernand Braudel could compare events to fireflies that shine enchantingly but are not able to truly illuminate the night.[74] In methodological passages of his *The Mediterranean and the Mediterranean World in the Age of Phillip* II, he urged historians to resist the charms of *l'histoire événementielle*. They should embrace the quest for new historical vistas fully detached from past actors' interests, illusions, passions, and myopias, modelled by the influence of emerging social scientific disciplines like geography. Braudel clarified that he did not consider himself to be an enemy of the event, and roughly one-third of his pioneering work is indeed an account centred on observable happenings. But he suggests that this part of the book plays no explanatory role whatsoever, insisting that 'the essentials of man's past' were to be searched for not in the domain of loud and volatile events but rather in silent and slower-changing structures.[75] In the 1970s, following this lead, Emmanuel Le Roy Ladurie saw

---

[71] Simiand, 'Historical Method and Social Science', 180, 209–10.
[72] See Iggers & Wang, *A Global History of Modern Historiography*, 157–66, 217–21, 241–3; Raphael, 'Die "Neue Geschichte"'; Sreedharan, *A Textbook of Historiography*, 231–80.
[73] Raphael, 'Die "Neue Geschichte"', 54–7.   [74] Braudel, *On History*, 10–11.
[75] Braudel, *The Mediterranean*, 18–21; 901–3.

the whole *Annales* tradition, to which he belonged, as feeding into the project of a '*histoire immobile*' ('motionless history') largely indifferent 'to what is happening on the surface'.[76]

French historians tended to adopt a colourfully polemical tone that makes them very quotable, but, as suggested, after 1945 comparable stances and approaches that aimed at turning historiography into a 'modernist' enterprise, a predominantly analytic science, became more and more disseminated. We are reminded here of the US cliometricians, the practitioners of historical prosopography, the critics of *Historismus* in West Germany, or of countless Marxist-inspired historians all over the world.[77] *Social history* is the methodological label that was most frequently used throughout the twentieth century to point to such attempts, as well as others, at redefining historical research and writing in dialogue with the social sciences. It tended to reject a good deal of the individualizing manners typical of the traditional historians of great men of politics and culture. Instead, it directed attention to group-related conditions and the general backgrounds that framed past lives, or to collective entities and their actions, patterns, and transformations.

However, despite the frequent polemical statements with which the 'new historians' battled for space amid methodological debates, they were not simply all about structures. Not every social history is a structural history: subject matters such as the trajectories of workers' associations or movements for women's rights tended to be studied under the label of social history, even when the dominant approach was sometimes that of the history of events. Besides, as Jürgen Kocka remarks, an uncompounded structural analysis would render only knowledge of possible events, not of real ones.[78] Social historians' antagonism to the historiographical tradition was not so radical as to divert many of them from the history of what was to that of what might have occurred. Hence, in their works we usually run into plenty of real events, notwithstanding the firm belief that these would not be well explained so long as the analysis did not find a way out of the *événementiel*.

Eventually, different traditions of social history did succeed in converting into methodological common sense the demand that historians should be sensitive to the complex ways events, actions, and characters are related to settings of different sorts. A good measure of this success can be taken from the fact that today the 'history of events' is often taken as a term of abuse.[79] Truth be told, in the large spectrum of contemporary historical cultures there are still

---

[76] Quoted in Dosse, 'Historical Event', 37–8.
[77] Iggers & Wang, *A Global History of Modern Historiography*, 250–70.
[78] Kocka, *Sozialgeschichte*, 74–5.   [79] Bösch, 'Das historische Ereignis'.

many eventful histories, but within the academic world one does not see scholars proudly introducing themselves as 'historians of events'.

3.2 Individuality and Repetitiveness

Having placed the yearnings for structural histories in a long-term perspective and then characterized their culmination in the practices and self-perceptions of many of the twentieth century's most innovative historians, we should now look more closely at the general idea of social structures that is presupposed in such developments. 'Structure' – to begin with a brief etymological note – has roots in the vocabulary of engineering, and in the seventeenth century biologists began using the word as a metaphor for the interdependence between the parts of a living body.[80] Marx, Durkheim, and Saussure were particularly important vectors in consolidating the application of the term to the social domain – even though many other strands in the history of the concept could easily be credited as relevant as well.

Marx employed the term 'structure' only occasionally in his writings, but the notion features in the above-quoted and, lately, very influential passage in the Preface to the *Contribution to the Critique of Political Economy*, in which he offers a summary of his basic views on history and social relations. Durkheim, for his part, made consistent use of the term in *The Rules of the Sociological Method*, and the strong echo found in this text was to a great extent determinant of the fate of the concept in twentieth-century social theory. Saussure, in turn, largely modelled his consequential concept of '*langue*' (language in terms of its abstract, recursive, shared rules as opposed to '*parole*' – speech – the singular, unrepeatable use of a language by an individual speaker) on Durkheim's notion of social facts. In his *Course in General Linguistics*, Saussure speaks of 'structure' only rarely and in a relatively modest sense, in reference to patterns in word formation or construction of sentences. When characterizing the solidified interconnections between signs that enable speech within a collective, he clearly favours the term 'system'. But his followers would, from the late 1920s, popularize his work as the cornerstone of a 'structural' or 'structuralist' programme in linguistics that would be enormously successful within and outside the discipline.[81]

By such and other paths, 'social structures' (as well as some parallel concepts, such as 'social facts', 'social patterns', or 'social systems') became a key notion in the modern social sciences. These would not exist, or would be very different from how they turned out to be, without the basic idea that relevant

---

[80] Chazel, 'Social Structure', 15233.
[81] Dosse, *History of Structuralism*, I, xxii, 44–5; Coseriu, *Sincronia, diacronia e historia*, 32–43.

aspects of the human world can only be addressed by shifting analytical attention from single individuals and their singular doings to more general frameworks of repetition within which we can say that events take place. An operative
definition would be that social structures serve as a very generic designation of
'almost any form of regularity or constraint in social life'.[82] The term points,
therefore, to what enables or compels individual actions, to recursive conditions
which in any case can hardly be shaped in a controlled way by actors at their
will.[83]

Such a definition, it is important to recall, is not meant as a starting point for
an exhaustive analytical theory of social structures. Its purpose is rather to
provide some phenomenological insight into a key implication carried by
many critiques of event-centred historiography and attempts to overcome it.
As mentioned, the approach I take seeks to stay in touch with historians'
methodological consciousness, and at the present juncture this entails acknow-
ledging that *social structures* and parallel concepts have tended not to be
defined in logically consistent ways by those who use them. Here, as elsewhere,
a somewhat metaphysical understanding is built upon rather loose conceptual
usages traceable in the historiographical world, and on the assumption that these
usages are indicative of the ways in which historians make sense of the past,
select aspects of it as their subject matter, formulate research questions, and
choose investigative methods. Attempts at providing more specific and logically rigorous definitions seem, in any case, fated to encounter formidable
obstacles. It is, as Sewell points out, quite difficult to explain what structures
are without resorting to the word in its very definition, or to synonyms like
'patterns', 'ways of acting', or 'circumstances'. 'Structure', he concludes, 'is
less a precise concept than a kind of founding or epistemic metaphor of social
scientific – and scientific – discourse'.[84] It is, we can add, a metaphor that brings
to the fore vertical relations among the constituents of the human world.
Accordingly, it configures this world as a space segmented in different layers,
the most interesting and causally relevant of which stay hidden beyond the
surface of immediate experience. Structure-oriented approaches assume, hence,
that proper understandings of social reality can only be reached when we find
analytical ways to descend down to its depths.[85]

The many forms of structural historiography that emerged from the late
nineteenth century onwards are united to the extent that they are all committed
to such vertical movements. By the same token, they also share mistrust of
historical explanations fixated on actions, ideas, and persons. Individual

---

[82] Martin, *Social Structures*, ix.
[83] Chazel, 'Social Structure', 15235; Haslanger, 'What Is a (Social) Structural Explanation?', 125–8.
[84] Sewell, *Logics of History*, 124–5.   [85] Megill, *Historical Knowledge*, 82.

thoughts and behaviour are then taken to be just superficial manifestations of processes or mechanisms that cannot be observed, so to say, with the naked eye. For modernist historians, a truly scientific history would only be inaugurated when one learned to address recursive aspects of past realities that cannot be conceived in terms of events. For this reason, Bloch, for instance, claimed, in the 1940s, that history 'is not only a science in movement'; it is 'also a science in its infancy'. Although history writing was a very old epistemic business, he found that most histories from the past were 'mere' narratives, not dissociated enough from myths and legends. They therefore lacked the level of legitimacy that was characteristic of other sciences. To turn things around, it was imperative that historians developed ways to 'penetrate beneath the mere surface of actions', and to take past factuality not so much as the subject of narratives but of other cognitive means.[86]

Like Bloch, most modernist historians did not endorse the mechanistic views of historical causation that former generations of positivists had embraced with enthusiasm. Nor were they sympathetic to the related search for putative laws of historical development. Yet they inhabited a diffusely scientistic metaphysical environment that positivism had much contributed to shape and that oriented them towards general or collective subjects of study, which were conceptualized under a variety of labels. The notion of *social structure* was not universally employed at the time, but it comprehends precisely this kind of object, endowed with a good, though indeterminate, degree of generality, duration, and stability, which is more or less hidden, invisible from the surface, in contradistinction to the unrepeatable, ephemeral, and superficial *event*.

The complex relationship between events and structural settings is a key thematic tension characteristic of countless, perhaps all, texts of history. But closer inspection soon reveals that the relation is always dependent on the mediation of a third metaphysical party, namely, the characters who initiate events, take part in them, live through them, and whose spaces of action, suffering, and thought are shaped and constrained by structures of different sorts. At this point, it may be useful to recall that both *characters* and *settings* fall under Megill's notion of *existents*, that this works as a counter-category to *events*, and that characters can be divided into *persons* and *social individuals*.[87] Emphasizing this last subdivision is important because it gives us a direct indication of the degree to which, since its beginnings, historiography has been about more than the actions, sufferings, and thoughts of individual human beings in the past. We do not need to go through many pages in Herodotus to find, for instance, a rebel *band* of nomadic Scythians crossing

---

[86] Bloch, *The Historian's Craft*, 11–15.   [87] See Section 1.

into Median territory, Megacles and Lycurgus uniting their supporters into a single *party* to evict Pisistratus from Athens, or *the Milesians* suffering defeats before the Lydian *army*.[88] Old and new histories often revolve around collectives such as ethnic groups, families, crowds, military units, governments, corporations, social classes, and many more. The term 'social individuals' was used by Danto to designate such entities,[89] which historians naturally take as agents or patients somehow endowed with consciousnesses, feelings, and intentions.

Social individuals fit the suit of existents and are locatable in the space between human persons and supra-individual settings. Yet what is intriguing about them is that they can play distinct roles in historical interpretations, sometimes simultaneously. There is a measure of convertibility between socio-cultural structures and social individuals – a feature represented by the two-pronged line in Figure 2. On the one hand, social individuals are characters in events, such as a social or an artistic movement defying established conventions, a corporation or a government facing bankruptcy, or an army unit winning or losing battles. But, on the other hand, in historical interpretations the same terms that name some abstract social individuals can also refer to settings. In this possibility, social individuals can be identified with the many sorts of structures that modernist historians learned to place at the centre of their analytic eye. 'Working class', for instance, can designate a collective character in a history text, but the term may also point to a setting that enables and constrains the behaviour of the individual human beings that constitute it as a social individual. The same applies to Braudel's Mediterranean, which was not only a 'non-people person' (in Jack Hexter's critical words),[90] but also a complex socio-geographic setting for events related to lower-level characters and entities.

Abstract social individuals can hence be identified with either collective characters or settings, or even with both simultaneously, but the notion is overstretched when extended towards large-scale events. Danto did so to emphasize that events such as the Thirty Years War result from the interaction of many different actors over a large period of time.[91] This, however, erases the boundary between happening and being. In other words, it conflicts with the assumption that events have no being; that they *are not* as they, rather, *happen to* beings.[92] In the basic metaphysical understanding I favour, social individuals are better addressed as existents and this automatically implies that they are not to be conflated with events.

---

[88] Herodotus, *The Histories*, 9, 25, 33.   [89] Danto, *Narration and Knowledge*, 258.
[90] Quoted in Megill, *Historical Knowledge*, 96.   [91] Danto, *Narration and Knowledge*, 258–9.
[92] See Romano, *Event and World*, 24–6.

Within this framework of relations traceable between the main content categories of historiography, another consequential feature is that persons are in many ways closer to events than they can be to structural settings. Historical events are conspicuously unique. They are unrepeatable and irrevocable just as an individual person is (or should be) irreplaceable and undeletable. The Fall of the Bastille only happened once, just as there was only one Qin Shi Huang, one Frida Kahlo, and one Martin Guerre – though in the latter case, notably studied by Natalie Zemon Davis, we could also say that, in a sense, there were two.[93]

It is true that also social structures are individualizable. 'The Italian Renaissance', Heinrich Rickert observed, 'is just as much a historical individual as Machiavelli'.[94] The statement applies to all sorts of contexts, structures, or institutions considered as higher-level individuals constituted by lower-level ones, like groups, persons, or objects.[95] Settings are complex results from social construction and as such they are unique and susceptible to change. However, historians and social scientists are often interested in settings not simply because of their uniqueness and changeability, but owing to a further quality that cannot be attributed to persons or events. Legal, political, economic, social, or symbolic systems are enablers of reiteration; they stimulate or compel that events of a certain kind come to pass. They are, in other words, patterns of repetition pervaded with a generality of the sort that events and persons lack. Individual persons' interactions in certain realms of social life tend to crystallize into such patterns, which, in turn, having reached a certain degree of crystallization, work as an immaterial means of inducing social reproduction, that is, repetition of similar interactions.[96] Social scientists, including social historians, model such recursive structures from different sorts of data as a way to synthetically grasp how individual agency, suffering, and thought in a society is simultaneously enabled and constrained by factors that no one person alone can wilfully determine. While analysing these factors, we tend not only to be concerned with their uniqueness, but also with the ways in which they embody regularities affecting different, sometimes numberless, human individuals.

Recurring patterns that affect persons, constraining or enabling events, are not exclusively of a social kind. There are also repetitions grounded in cosmological, geological, geographic, climatic, biological, or anthropological factors

---

[93] Davis, *The Return of Martin Guerre*.   [94] Rickert, *The Limits of Concept Formation*, 108.

[95] Epstein (*The Ant Trap*, 36–49, 129–31) questions what he diagnoses as a broad consensus among contemporary social ontologists according to which facts about individuals globally supervene upon social facts. On the neglected role of non-human parts in social wholes, see Elder-Vass, 'Material Parts in Social Structures'.

[96] Martin, *Social Structures*, 1–3.

that can be relevant for historical understanding.[97] Some structural histories give ample room to such conditions, without necessarily resorting to naturalistic reductionisms. Many contemporary environmental historians do so, even when they problematize the old intellectual habit of rigidly distinguishing the natural from the social, the cultural, or the historical.[98] As a rule, nonetheless, social history focuses on relatively durable configurations that are more directly dependent on human ingenuity. It tends to be drawn primarily to structures that set the social stage, so to speak, on which, in each historical conjuncture, events unfold. 'Social' here is an umbrella term for human-made conditions of different sorts that affect collective experience and that are put together simply because they would resist being classified as 'natural'. In any case, the underlying thought behind all forms of structural history seems to be that histories based on events are much too incomplete, and hence should be either supplemented or replaced by those that spotlight natural and especially non-natural settings.

3.3 Moving beyond Dichotomies

As we have seen, *histories of events* were never purely recollective or descriptive, as the explanations embedded in them always presuppose the existence in the past of general, recurring patterns. If we search hard, we may find in them different versions of the intuition that in order for a unique event to occur, several repetitive structures must be at work. As Reinhart Koselleck notes, even the most pronounced histories of events imply structures as 'conditions of possibility' for actions and interactions. Events are enabled by already existing, intersubjective, and relatively durable structures that can be spotted *in* them. What happens may be radically new and surprising, or foster social creativity and structural changes, but, as Koselleck puts it, it cannot be 'so revolutionary that it would cease to be dependent on pre-existing structures of repetition'. To stress this, one should notice, is not the same as to make a case for cyclical or developmental laws understood in teleological or fatalistic fashion.[99] Since Droysen and Rickert, at least, it should come as no surprise that in historical knowledge we encounter various forms of generality that have nothing to do with law-like postulations.[100]

---

[97] Koselleck, *Vom Sinn und Unsinn der Geschichte*, 96–114; Koselleck, *Begriffsgeschichten*, 32–55.

[98] Mauldin, 'Environmental History'.

[99] Koselleck, *Zeitschichten*, 21–2, 45–7, 66–7; Koselleck, *Vergangene Zukunft*, 144–9; Koselleck, *Vom Sinn und Unsinn der Geschichte*, 99–100, 114.

[100] Droysen, *Historik*, 27–30; Rickert, *The Limits of Concept Formation*, 115–16.

Structural histories, in turn, privilege the settings, not least because they emphasize how much individual agency is socially circumscribed, shaped, dependent, or determined. They aim at drawing profound and explicit consequences from the fact that every new event can only come to pass under such structural conditions of possibility. However, while structural histories strongly privilege social entities and causes, they cannot do without studying, referencing, or at least presupposing, events and persons. Hypothetically, perhaps, an over-the-top structuralist historian might manage to avoid the use of proper names, thus generating a very abstract text. But it would be hard to view their conclusions about the functioning and transformation of structures as a product of historical thought if those could not be validated or exemplified by reference to singular events and persons.

Because of these and other interdependencies, historians have learned to defy rigid dichotomies which stipulate that they should stick to either events or structures. In fact, a key feature of many of the best works of history published in recent decades is that they are neither purely structural nor purely *événementiel*, but both, in ever differently shaped combinations.[101] Moving back and forth from particular events to persons and social individuals, and then to structures and structural changes, they depict interplays between these factors under given configurations of time and space. This is in line with the well-established tendency in late twentieth-century social theory to narrow the divide between agency and structure with the aid of concepts and models that are able to capture the complex interrelatedness between them in the social world – as in Anthony Giddens' theory of structuration or Pierre Bourdieu's social praxeology, to mention only two very prominent examples.[102]

When it comes to theorizations by historians, Koselleck's notion of multiple historical temporalities can be seen as a far-reaching elaboration of the same concerns. Taking inspiration from Braudel – though without sharing his reservations with regard to the event as a metahistorical category – Koselleck canvasses the different levels of interrelated structural conditions that make an event possible, and the varying tempos at which change in these conditions is processed.[103] With his geologically modelled notion of the 'sediments of time', he drives at a temporalization of our ways of perceiving structures; we could think of it as a sort of *eventisation*, as it results in structures being analytically treated in ways that used to be reserved for events. Koselleck's approach to historical times emphasizes how events and structures are entangled without fully blurring the borders between them. Structures then come out

---

[101] Dosse, 'Historical Event', 40–2; Pereira, 'A história', 64–7. [102] Peters, *Percursos*, 9–30.
[103] Koselleck, *Zeitschichten*, 22.

as dynamic and changeable, while the links between events and their structural 'conditions of possibility' are specified. This view is tied to an attempt to defuse another rigid dichotomy that haunted twentieth-century social sciences: the one between synchrony and diachrony.

An equally nuanced treatment of the issue is found in the neo-structuralist theory of events developed by Sewell, in which historical events are seen as distinguished precisely by their power to induce reconfigurations in social structures.[104] The idea that structures set the stage for events is almost unavoidable, but Sewell helps us to remain aware of some complications that come with such scenic metaphors. Above all, he emphasizes that no setting is composed of just one single structure. In the social worlds of the past and in the present, persons belong simultaneously to different social groups, have multiple collective identities, and get along with different orders of codes and rules. Structures combine with other structures, can be categorized according to their different levels of depth or degrees of crystallization, or can be seen as substructures of higher-level structures. Some – as we will see – are perceived as such by the people living under them, while others remain outside the reach of their consciousnesses. For all this, it is very hard to say that an event takes place within a single structural domain without performing a great exercise in abstraction. Structures, hence – as Sewell emphasizes to mark the fact that they are asymmetric, intersecting, overlapping, and transposable – are best spoken of in the plural.[105]

Sewell's and Koselleck's ruminations on the relationship between events and structures are exceptional, not only for their depth and insightfulness, but also because of the more basic reason that they delve into subjects that have been largely absent from contemporary historical theories. Even though varieties of non-event-centric histories have been in existence for a long time, the role of structures and other collective entities in historiography has increasingly received little attention, especially in English-speaking theoretical circles. The issue, however, is quite close to questions that have never ceased to be studied extensively by social theorists and philosophers of the social sciences. The subfield of social ontology, for instance, has established itself in recent decades as a hub of inquiries into the nature of the social, and the entities of the social world.[106] But, to date, insights and conclusions by social ontologists have by and large passed under the radar of historical theorists. Here, a dialogue that could further the understanding of historical knowledge is inhibited, I think, in consequence of our tendency to assume that histories are about events in an automatic and disproportionate way.

---

[104] Sewell, *Logics of History*, 197–270.   [105] Ibid., 143, 204–11.
[106] Epstein, 'Social Ontology'.

In this section, I have sketched how the history of historiography during the first half of the twentieth century was marked by a conflict between traditional and modernist approaches. I stressed that the latter went in different directions, but were united on the minimization of the epistemic value of events. As modernist historians attempted to move historical knowledge's centre of gravity towards non-*événementiel* facts, the notion of structure presented itself as a good synthesis of the new type of objects many of them had in mind; objects hosted at dimensions of social reality distinguished by attributes that are absent in singular events, such as depth, stability, or repeatability. Subsections 3.2 and 3.3 initiated a theoretical review of social structures, understood as a major content category in historiography; this will continue and be expanded upon in the remainder of this Element. As I have sometimes signalled, histories may be attentive to structurally shaped existents of various kinds and magnitudes. Until the late 1960s, social historians tended to privilege large, unconscious patterns construable on the basis of economic or demographic data, to the detriment of experience-proximate or consciousness-enabling structures, in most cases of smaller scales. Yet, since the 1970s, the latter have been pieced together and reconceived under what is sometimes called the 'anthropological concept of culture', and soon enough a renewed orientation towards the cultural world was visible also in historical research. It brought with it a renewed sensitivity to events, actors, and subjective experience, but this by no means meant the end of structural histories. The next section will comprise a theoretical examination of such symbolic structures, as well as a historical overview of how structural historiography was transformed in order to accommodate them as thematic priorities.

4 Symbolic Webs

4.1 Meanings and Resources

So far, we have considered basically two types of settings: the less human-related ones, which shall remain underexplored here, and the more anthropocentric ones, lumped together under the term 'social structures', which have been discussed at some length. However, the catalogue of historiography's basic content categories introduced in Section 1 includes another sub-variant of human-centred settings under the heading 'symbolic webs'. It is now timely to inquiry into these, to ascertain how they do or do not fit with the points just made with respect to social structures.

A way of starting such an exercise is to consider that 'structural' may refer to either material conditions related to resources or to semiotic, meaning-related contexts. This asymmetry is frequently evoked by the use of 'structure' and

'culture' as oppositive concepts denoting substantially different kinds of frameworks for events. Such a way of speaking highlights a distinction that, as will be
seen, had its importance and justification in the history of historical and social
research. But, at the same time, it masks the extent to which cultural phenomena
bear structural traces and how often they have been treated structurally by
anthropologists and historians. It is, furthermore, insensitive to the circumstance that the ascent of cultural history in the late twentieth century was
marked not only by challenges and critiques launched against established
social-historical practices and postulates. In effect, a large majority of cultural-
historical productions stood in a tense and creative continuity vis-à-vis older
forms of structural history. The significance of these continuities and complementarities is such that one could say that cultural history belongs in the great
family of social histories. Or perhaps, looking into the history of historiography
more broadly, it is also plausible to reverse the statement and take social
histories as part of the greater family of cultural history.[107] The intricate
relationship between both has prompted disagreements over which one is the
chicken and which one, the egg.

The dilemma is partially fuelled by the acknowledgement that in real social
life the material and the symbolic can be so intertwined that theoretical attempts
to disentangle them become hopeless. We are familiar with people being
categorized as human resources, material things having symbolic values,
expressed meanings being enmeshed in material supports (such as a canvass
or an electronic device's screen), and so on. With this in mind, and speaking
from a social-theoretical perspective, Sewell reconceives structures as sets of
semiotic schemas and material resources that 'mutually imply and sustain each
other over time'.[108] According to him (and to Giddens, on whose definitions
Sewell elaborates) the interrelationship of meaning-generative schemas (shared
rules, beliefs, principles of action, concepts, metaphors, attitudes, etc.) and
social resources (human or non-human) endows structures with a constitutive
duality that must be handled with great care in any first-order social analysis.[109]

Yet, a brief look into the history of historiography shows that the duality at the
centre of such a theory of structures has not been observed by practicing
historians in a proportional manner. Until recently, structural histories tended
to focus on either resources or schemas, often without carefully considering the
complex relations between these two poles. To put this in a rough synthesis,
mid-twentieth-century leading social historians tended to be attracted to social
resources, as illustrated by the large number of interpretations focused on

---

[107] Raphael, *Geschichtswissenschaft im Zeitalter der Extreme*, 173–5.
[108] Sewell, *Logics of History*, 137.   [109] Ibid., 128–33.

economic cycles, demographic fluxes, industrialization processes, and geography-related changes that were then produced. In the last decades of the century, on the other hand, more and more historians turned to cultural schemas graspable through the medium of notions such as mentalities, representations, concepts, or ideology.

Much of the frequently evoked opposition between the social and the cultural is rooted in the dissimilarity between resources and meaning-generative schemas. As with the former, the latter distinction indeed includes some degree of artificiality and significant grey areas, but there are also key situations in which it counts as more than an excusable simplification. In a far-reaching assessment, Huizinga once noted that since the end of the thirteenth century Western European societies had been marked by the ascending economic power of the middle classes. Even so, from the late Middle Ages up to the seventeenth century, values, symbols, and sensibilities originally attached to the feudal nobility, as for instance the ideal of knighthood, remained socially pre-eminent almost everywhere in Europe. In this context, a very important dissonance between two large structural domains became visible. As Huizinga put it, 'the life form of the nobility still retains its relevance over society long after the nobility as social structure had lost its dominant meaning'. Here, he was capturing a mismatch between the material configurations of a society and the patterns of symbolization and knowledge its members resorted to in order to make sense of the world. Such disjunctions are significant enough to justify the coexistence of markedly different historiographical approaches to settings or structurally shaped objects. From a resource-centred perspective, late-medieval or early modern people's special fondness for cultural forms of the feudal nobility could simply be disregarded as wrong-headed. It is addressed as an error perpetuated by the contemporaries, which the historian aims at undoing – for instance, by tracing slow changes in the structures of medieval economies that escaped peoples' awareness at the time.

Huizinga did not deny the validity of such approaches that bypass the subjective perceptions of past agents, but he insisted that if we want to know what cultural life in the past was like, then we must take the contemporaries' 'illusions' much more seriously. 'We have to be aware that the illusion itself retained its value as truth for those who lived it.'[110] What we have here is a separable structural domain of reality that hosts the patterns connected to what past people felt, believed, knew, or thought they knew.

It does not matter much whether the contrast between resources and symbols is to be discarded, strengthened, refined, or merely acknowledged as a useful

---

[110] Huizinga, *The Autumn of the Middle Ages*, 61–2.

heuristic device – though the first two are definitely not the best available options. Much more important for our purposes – which, to recall, is more phenomenological than logical or social-theoretical – is that the distinction had a great impact on the division of labour in the social sciences (functionalism and Marxism, for instance, favouring resources, whereas phenomenological sociology and cultural anthropology focused on symbols). The tension that it featured was strongly felt within the historical discipline, serving as a source not only of sterile polemics but also of methodological innovations.[111] In other words, the distinction between material and symbolic structures corresponds very well to differences in terms of ways of building concepts, selecting objects, and employing methods activated in different traditions of historical (and also social scientific) scholarship. To reach a wider understanding of such differences we need to bring the analysis back into a more consistent historical perspective.

4.2 The Cultural Turn

The first wave of structural histories in the twentieth century split in many different directions. But a clear preference for resources rather than meanings was traceable, and, in effect, by mid-century economic and demographic approaches established themselves as mainstream orientations in many subfields and national landscapes. Attention to populational oscillations, revenue systems, labour relations, mechanisms of social stratification, and class conflicts, among other phenomena, stimulated a formidable broadening of historiographical interests. It became increasingly self-evident that histories could be about much more than the actions and accomplishments of a few 'great men'. Modernist historians were developing a number of ways to widen the scope of historical interpretation into previously uncharted social spaces. They were now able to go beyond the relatively small political or cultural elites in respect of which they accused their predecessors of being confined.[112]

This expansion of historiographical horizons was, however, partially dependent on a crucial material condition: the availability of sources. During most of human history, the vast majority of people, including especially underprivileged people, were illiterate. As a result, later historians can only rely, at best, on very scarce direct testimonies of how most of the people in the past perceived themselves and the world.[113] This inherited condition was a key element that dragged modernist historians away from the experiences of past people and

---

[111] Serna & Pons, *La historia cultural*, 23–5; Welskopp, 'Die Sozialgeschichte'.

[112] Sewell, *Logics of History*, 27–9.

[113] Davis, *The Return of Martin Guerre*, 1–2; Ginzburg, *The Cheese and the Worms*, xiii–xx.

closer to non-narrative modes of 'analysis', especially in the 1950s and 1960s. Given the paucity of direct materials that could be used to canvass the thoughts and actions of underprivileged individuals, several historians turned to statistical methods, as well as macro-sociological concepts and models, to shed light on general patterns that shaped many individual lives.

The expansion of the social scope of historical knowledge was not without its costs. It required a reliance on de-individualizing, consciousness-distant, if not experience-hostile approaches, with which a growing dissatisfaction emerged from the mid-1970s onwards. Social historians of more recent pasts started to supplement or contrast statistical data with information generated by means of questionnaires and oral-historical methods.[114] Edward Thompson became an especially authoritative role model for those who had increasing doubts about the powers of quantification, as well as complaints about the determinism of cherished social theories – especially those shaped by orthodox Marxism. Many historians took *The Making of the English Working Class* (1963) as a great example of how to write 'history from below' while focusing on subjective experiences and the relative autonomy of individuals as agents.[115] The controversy between interpretivist and quantitativist approaches in the social sciences also began to take a decisive shape, fuelled by the ascent of consciousness-oriented, phenomenological approaches in sociology and, with greater effects, cultural anthropology. Clifford Geertz was a key figure in this shift. He took the symbolic as crucial to the understanding of social life and regarded *culture* as the province of the symbolic. In his famous definition, the concept of culture 'denotes an historically transmitted pattern of meanings embodied in symbols, a system of inherited conceptions expressed in symbolic forms by means of which men communicate, perpetuate, and develop their knowledge about and attitudes toward life'.[116]

It is important to note that not all previous and posterior works in cultural history and cultural anthropology have stuck to this relatively unambiguous and rather 'structuralist' definition. The semantics of 'culture' may also lead historians beyond what is more immediately symbolic; for instance, into human-made extensions of the natural world like technical instruments and functional objects. We may then speak of housing, clothing, food, farming, fishing cultures, and much more. Here, the opposition between the material and the symbolic recedes into the background, being replaced by the tension between the natural and the artificial; 'culture' designates this non-natural, human-made domain. From this perspective, Justo Serna and Anaclet Pons claim that 'tools,

---

[114] Raphael, *Geschichtswissenschaft im Zeitalter der Extreme*, 180.
[115] Bell, 'Total History and Microhistory', 266–7.
[116] Geertz, *The Interpretation of Cultures*, 89.

prostheses, and meanings constitute culture', thus accommodating the fact that many cultural histories are less centred on symbolic forms and goods than on culture as the domain of human-made artificiality.[117]

Moreover, cultural forms and goods were never surveyed exclusively as nodes within structural webs. Historical approaches to themes pertaining to religions, art forms, moral or political thought, or the sciences, among others, can underline what is special, surprising, transformative in them, instead of what can be seen as pattern-related instances. Especially (though not exclusively) in intellectual history, interpreters are often interested in explaining how works, ideas, theories, and so on individually came to light and were conveyed, received, adapted, neglected, or forgotten. They may be attentive to various kinds of 'contexts' but focus on singularities inherent in consciously devised cultural products that are deemed particularly original, enlightening, relevant, or that proved very influential. Such products seem to have a kind of value that resists attempts to entirely dissolve them into structural frameworks; a value that stems not so much from their contexts of origin as from either their context-transcendent capacities or from later contexts, including the context where the interpretation itself takes place.

There are, hence, interpretative situations that call for less structural or contextualist, more thought-immanent and singularizing approaches to meanings and symbolic forms. We come close here to the history of events, for, as mentioned, an event too can be the focus of a historical interpretation because it is perceived as radically new or transformative, or due to its relevance for the interpreter and their aimed audience. Moreover, as in the case of events, sometimes contextualist approaches to the cultural world prove insufficient. As already discussed, Romano's conclusions in his phenomenological inquiry into 'world-establishing events' – that is, occurrences that 'radically upend their contexts' – apply nicely to the characterization of radically new or influential, self-consciously devised ideas; to 'intellectual events', as Martin Jay proposes they may be called.[118] Figure 2 takes this into account by placing *thoughts* as a content category besides *actions* and *sufferings*, and under the generic heading of *events*.

As can be seen, cultural histories can take different forms depending on the standpoint, epistemic interests, metaphysical assumptions, and methodological choices of those who write them. But it is indisputable that the Geertzian approach had a decisive impact on the historiographical landscape of the 1970s and 1980s. It was a powerful propeller of a new sensitivity to past agency,

---

[117] Serna & Pons, *La historia cultural*, 18.
[118] Romano, *Event and World*, 38; Jay, 'Historical Explanation and the Event', 567–8. See Section 2.2.

its symbolic underpinnings, and the forms of subjective knowledge and experience involved in it. This new sensitivity can be conceived as the main fruit of a 'cultural turn' which, as everywhere in the humanities, was accomplished in diverse directions.[119] A distinctive feature of these new styles of cultural interpretation was doubtfulness about forms of causal explanation that were typical of former traditions of social analysis. As Barbara Weinstein points out, in historiography the cultural turn entailed a 'decline of causation', sometimes followed by the conversion of former causal explanations into 'raw material for discourse analysis'. Yet, as she also notes, causal relations and narrative explanations of how meaning systems were configured and reconfigured over time are often very present in cultural-historical interpretations, as undiscussed and sometimes unconscious assumptions bearing the status of historiographical common sense.[120]

In line with the 'cultural turn' were proclamations of the 'return of the event' and the 'return of narrative' issued by historians and cultural theorists from the early 1970s onwards. Various meanings were assigned to such heralded comebacks, but in no way was the case made for a simple rehabilitation of old-style histories of events. We could perhaps say that these proclamations attest that the modernist drive towards structural phenomena was enriched and made more complex through its reconciliation with the more traditional attention to smaller-scale events. The proclamations also suggest that a new outlook on events was emerging, within which events were taken not as end results to be explained but as memory landmarks for future reinterpretations and reappropriations. The Braudelian divide between events and the *longue durée* was thus to be closed, as the former were no longer automatically identified with occurrences lacking temporal extension. The mnemohistorical approaches mentioned in Section 2.2 promoted the discovery that some events have a *longue durée* of their own, which is connected to their shifting meanings within different temporal contexts.[121]

Having been substantially downgraded by powerful though widely differing traditions such as structuralism, functionalism, and Marxism, 'the subject', too, was somehow resurrected in the methodological imaginations of social scientists and historians. Nonetheless, as in the case of events, the new focus was not so much on individual action, suffering, or thought as on the relationship between persons and social structures, and on the mediation of this relation by theoretical and especially practical knowledge of social rules and informal conventions. Again, it is not that structures or structural thinking were abandoned; rather,

---

[119] In *Cultural Turns*, Bachmann-Medick refers to series of associated 'turns': performative, literary, post-colonial, translational, spatial, and iconic.

[120] Weinstein, 'History without a Cause?', 72–8.

[121] Dosse, 'Historical Event'; Revel, *Proposições*, 86–7, 93–5; Tamm, 'Introduction', 6–8.

they were reconnected to the level of personal, subjective experience in an unprecedentedly intensive way. Arguing against both the empiricism characteristic of psychologist approaches to culture and the abstractness of structuralist and functionalist ones, Geertz insisted that anthropology should aim at being an actor-oriented sort of knowledge, though definitively not at simply reproducing actors' perspectives. General 'cultural forms' could be elucidated, but only through an especially calibrated way of social description that takes into account that such forms only find articulation 'through the flow of behaviour', that is, concrete actions and interactions. 'Whatever, or wherever, symbol systems "in their own terms" may be, we gain empirical access to them by inspecting events, not by arranging abstracted entities into unified patterns.'[122] Attention to similar tensions and balances between general and particular, macro and micro, actor and observer, structures and events is crucial for assessing the epistemic accomplishments of pioneering late-twentieth-century cultural historians like Natalie Zemon Davis, Carlo Ginzburg, Alain Corbin, and so many others.

Around the year 2000, the turn to culture had left permanent marks even in the traditionally more event-centred domain of political history. This was traceable, for instance, in the popularity of a concept like 'political culture', or in the coinage of methodological labels such as 'new political history' or 'cultural history of politics'.[123] In his three-volume overview of the history of the Third Reich, Richard Evans commented that in the 1970s and 1980s, under the influence of social-historical modes of analysis, scholarship on his subject had widely disregarded real human beings in favour of large-scale structures and processes. In his own work, he wanted, he claimed, 'to put individuals back into the picture', and in fact he attempted to do so by, among other things, extensively drawing on biographical materials from contemporary characters both famous and obscure.[124] In Evans' case, the endeavour was mixed with a self-aware 'return' to a chiefly narrative mode of presentation, and yet his was no longer a clear-cut history of events.[125] The genies of structural analysis and cultural-historical interpretation had been out of the bottle for too long, and they could not simply be put back in.

4.3 Awareness of Settings

One crucial circumstance that was certainly felt, though not always theoretically discussed, by those who promoted the 'cultural turn' in historiography concerns the relationship between abstract structures and the actual people

---

[122] Geertz, *The Interpretation of Cultures*, 15–17.
[123] Mergel, 'Kulturgeschichte der Politik'; Pedersen, 'What Is Political History Now?'.
[124] Evans, *The Coming of the Third Reich*, xix.   [125] See Section 5.2.

who lived 'in' them. Did structural settings belong in the experiential worlds of past actors, or are they simply projected upon such worlds *ex post facto* by interpreters? Are structures, as analytical tools, in a continuum as regards the experience of past people or can structural analysts simply disregard past forms of consciousness and even run counter to them? These questions have profound methodological, metaphysical, and even ethical resonances. Engaging with them can help us understand the unease about earlier para-digms of structural historiography that many cultural historians expressed in the last decades of the twentieth century.

It goes without saying that individual persons do not perceive the existence of structures in the same way as they can see an event being enacted or suffered by someone. The settings in which people act are neither observable nor audible, at least not in the literal way a carnival party, a general strike, or the bombing of a bridge are discernible. Even so, past people who feature in history texts belonged in families, dealt with organizations, were members of groups, citizens of states, and, crucially, they knew that this was so. They were knowledgeably parts in social wholes of various sizes, just as historians, analysts of historiography, and pretty much everyone else in the present knows that they live their lives in relation to groups and institutions. But not all structural framings are within the reach of contemporaries' knowledge. People can be parts in structural wholes without knowing it, or without having a reasonably clear perception of it. Some social patterns, we could say, are very far removed from the subjective experiences of people living under them. They call for analytical resources and modes of thinking that are not available to a large majority of individuals in a society, or that will only be available to future analysts. Other features or patterns will only be construed as such retroactively, by historians who know about impacts and effects unknowable to the contemporaries.

Common to all these situations is that structures or the social-creative processes leading their establishment or change are addressed by retrospective or external 'observers' with the aid of theoretical models.[126] The kind of knowledge that emerges from such situations departs from any form of social intuition or self-perception that contemporary people (or at least a large majority of them) could have had. During the first waves of historiographical modernism, as we have seen, structurally oriented histories were concerned with neither particular individuals per se, nor the cultural constellations underpinning subjective perceptions and expressions. We could say that persons were important inasmuch as they could be seen as occupying nodes

---

[126] Danto, *Narration and Knowledge*, 264, 281–2.

in social structures, and especially when such structures were unintentionally instantiated by them.[127] The structures addressable as means or ends of historical explanations tended, therefore, to be 'external' vis-à-vis the experiential horizons of past individuals: geographic and demographic patterns; hierarchies of wealth; occupational distributions; inheritance, taxation, land tenure systems, and so on.[128] The conceptualization of such abstract objects by historians was premised on temporal, spatial, or societal forms of distanciation, leading to retroactive theories and interpretations that were alien to the conceptual and interpretative universes of the societies studied. For many, all this seemed necessary to implement the agenda of a non-event-centric approach that could give history the kind of epistemic legitimacy many branches of social science were assumed to have attained. Such a tendency was fully in line with what Giddens diagnosed as the great Marxist–functionalist consensus that characterized mid-twentieth-century social theory: the view that human behaviour results from social structures of which actors cannot themselves be aware.[129]

But the symbols and meanings to which the cultural turn directed the attention of historians are in all cases at the heart of human experience. They cannot be regarded as extrinsic to past people's representations and self-perceptions. At the same time, however, meanings and symbols in a given social configuration are mobilized within webs bestowed with structural features. It is for this reason that there can be structural histories focused on the symbolic, that is, on settings that are proximate to contemporaries' experience. 'Cultural history' is a good general label for them even though, as mentioned, the term must not be imprisoned within this definition. In a very broad understanding, cultural history deals with patterns that mediate people's self- and world-experience. Such patterns underpin individuals' sense and images of the world, of others, and of themselves. They therefore stand for structures of which people in the past had some sort of knowledge. In other words, in sharp contrast to the structural patterns at the centre of traditional approaches to economic or demographic history, cultural historians privilege consciousness-proximate structures. This intrinsic link with individual awareness is a key factor that explains why culture-oriented research is more friendly to human agency and more distant from deterministic assumptions concerning it than former structuralist, functionalist, or Marxist counterparts.

---

[127] See Haslanger, 'What Is a (Social) Structural Explanation?', 121; Ritchie, 'Social Structures and the Ontology of Social Groups', 408.

[128] These examples are borrowed from Sewell, *Logics of History*, 28.

[129] Giddens, *The Constitution of Society*, xix.

Although the symbolic is inextricably connected to the way persons from the past (as well as the present) perceive themselves and their worlds – that is, to subjective experience – meaning-related settings are also *objective* in a mentionable sense. They consist of shared structures of repetition endowed with some degree of stability, and they too impose constraints on actors. Webs of meaning that we can analytically allocate in domains such as language, myth, popular culture, religion, morality, science, and others therefore exhibit a tricky ambivalence. They are subject-bounded, sometimes subjectivity-constitutive, while also being objective in the sense that events, even those that do more than reproduce or instantiate such symbolic structures, are framed and limited by them. In any case, we are dealing with settings that cannot be simply objective for even more reasons than those at play in the case of unconscious structures. Adapting a comment by Ernst Cassirer, one could say that they are 'neither one-sidedly subjective nor one-sidedly objective', for they rather effect 'a new mediation, a distinctive reciprocal determination' between objective imitation and subjective expression.[130]

The distinction between unconscious and conscious structures finds a special justification in the circumstance that, after all, we ourselves depend on relatively stable symbolic forms in order to know all kinds of structures and events, as well as everything else. Consciousness-proximate cultural forms and goods lie at the basis of our knowledge faculties, and without them there actually could be no subjectivity in a strong sense. But like the contrast between material and symbolic structures, with which it bears a connection, the frontier between the unconscious and the conscious is marked by a large grey area instead of a clear-cut borderline. What is more, the division cannot be stabilized once and for all. Structural historiography and other forms of social analysis often direct attention to settings and processes that evaded the awareness of people living through them. What was socially unconscious in the past, however, can become conscious in the present, exactly by featuring as objects in epistemic acts. In contemporary societies, as an effect of a long-term, continuous stream of historical and social scientific knowledge production, social features and facts that used to pass unknown are now well mapped. The structurally bound mindsets enabling the awareness of such phenomena became part of the stock of social knowledge shared among members of different collectives in and outside the academic world.

Not least because of the cumulative effect of the work of historians and social scientists, individual persons can, for instance, see themselves as belonging to a social class or a statistical cohort, or acknowledge that they live under a certain

---

[130] Cassirer, *The Philosophy of Symbolic Forms*, I, 23.

type of state or economic order. Social-scientifically enabled perceptions like these can change the way people think and act, and hence have profound consequences on the very reality that is to be interpreted by human scientists. In this way, subjective cognition of patterns of social life itself becomes an objective factor of social life. This shows that historical and social scientific knowledge is not detached from the subjects and issues it is about, and how powerful its social impact can be – even if this cannot be measured by the technology-oriented standards that often apply to natural-scientific theories and findings.[131]

The discussion, in this section, of some key thematic features of cultural history has been an essential step in broadening our view of the intersection between events and structures in historiography. We have seen how not only subjectivity-distant, unconscious, and material structures but also experience-proximate, knowledgeable, and symbolic ones can be the focus of historians, and how privileging cultures entails specific methodological situations within the framework of structural historiography. Altogether, the foregoing sections on events, social structures, and symbolic webs constitute a tentative inquiry into tensions and complementarities between dissimilar modes of researching and writing history – modes connected, in short, to plural historical pasts. In the remainder of this Element, I will explore consequences that may follow from taking the heterogeneity of historical pasts seriously in such a vein. The four interrelated considerations on, respectively, methodology, explanation, exemplification, and narrative will set the argument developed hitherto in connection with some classical and recent debates about the constitution of historical knowledge.

5 Some Ramifications

5.1 Methodological Pluralism

Reduced to its very basics, the main message conveyed so far is that what we call 'the past' comprises, at least, persons and their thoughts, actions, and sufferings; events of many sorts and sizes; different kinds of structures and social individuals; and eventful processes leading to socio-cultural emergences, changes, and disappearances. This list of types of events and existents that are usually privileged in histories does not claim to be exhaustive or conclusive. But it is sufficiently comprehensive to put a damper on any lingering hopes of a single, all-inclusive historical method that could sustain a strong sense of identity across the historical discipline. There is no doubt that the community of academic historians has long been a very diverse one, and not only because it comprises so many heterogeneous

---

[131] Giddens, *The Constitution of Society*, xxxii–xxxv, 348–54; Peters, *Percursos*, 243–51.

sub-communities, themselves shaped by different histories, cultural backgrounds, and socio-politico challenges. An important dimension of what Pomian once called historiography's 'irreducible plurality' connects to the metaphysical asymmetries and methodological variations to which I have drawn attention.[132] Such variations and asymmetries give us strong grounds for speaking more of histories in the plural than we usually do.

'Pluralism', in this context, turns out to be a very special keyword. It points simultaneously to a fact about the current state of historical studies and to a norm as to how these should be assessed in reflective contexts. Seen as a whole, historiography is already plural, and for more than one reason. The most obvious is encapsulated in Goethe's memorable observation that 'world history must from time to time be re-written';[133] that is, in the now widely accepted view that interpretations of what was or what happened are strongly shaped by interpreters' temporal, geographical, cultural, political, or moral situatedness. Still, in speaking of 'plural pasts' or historiography's 'pluralism', I am not primarily concerned with such simultaneously subjective and social epistemological connections. My focus is rather on the objective pole of the process of historical knowledge; on the kinds of content privileged in it. Plurality in historiography, I claim, derives in no small measure from metaphysical and metaphysically entwined methodological circumstances. Histories adjusted to more or less the same spatial-temporal coordinates may sharply contrast with each other not only because they were written by different persons, who – within different temporal and social contexts, based on different sets of beliefs, moral values and emotions, and abiding by different presentational codes – select and arrange past events differently. Events, on full examination, might turn out to be not all that historians address, select, combine, or bypass, as their attention may be captured by existents of different kinds as well.

An important consequence of relieving events of their conventional status as the prototypical kind of content in histories is therefore an irrevocable methodological pluralism. This, in my view, is not only a fact to be stated, but also a fruitful condition to be both carefully theorized and practically cultivated. It is by now no mystery that such a mix of factual assertions and value judgements about metaphysical and methodological diversity in historiography informs the general goal towards which the previous surveys on events, social structures, and symbolic webs, taken together, have been moving.

Historical theory, broadly understood, is an obvious venue for setting such a goal, not least for the very reason that historiographical practice, most of the time, is unconcerned, perhaps even incompatible, with agendas such as the analysis and promotion of methodological pluralism. Historians have little reason to fully

---

[132] Pomian, *Sur l'histoire*, 392–8.   [133] Goethe, *Zur Farbenlehre*, II, 238.

embrace the kind of methodological agnosticism to which I have deliberately tried to stick for the purpose of this analysis. The great majority of them are primarily interested in generating knowledge about the past, not knowledge about historical knowledge. Of course, historians are well capable of methodological self-reflection, as the ideas discussed in the foregoing sections illustrate. But it is undeniable that, when pondering on methodology, they tend to turn to the methods they are familiar with, as well as to competing methods against which they intend to demonstrate the superiority of their own. To write, and to write polemically, about which should be the best approach to solve a given set of problems or to illuminate a thematic domain is not only excusable, but sometimes also a necessary condition for advancing historical knowledge. Yet historians' methodological discussions frequently run the risk of turning into self-interested attempts to claim an imaginary 'historicity prize'. Whenever, in self-reflective or comparative texts and speeches, scholars come close to validating this caricature, they are acting out of a monistic premise that is very different from the pluralistic one of which I am stressing the merits here.

In this somewhat agnostic way of approaching different, often concurrent, historiographical paradigms, the issue of judging which methodological approach or which type of content would be the most scientific then recedes into the background. By skipping over questions such as whether, in the abstract, histories that privilege existents are better than those that focus on events (or vice versa), we may gain a way of talking non-polemically and yet comparatively about different interpretations and interpretative traditions. As a matter of course, theorists of historiography are much less cognizant of the methodological and substantive particulars involved in the generation of first-order historical knowledge. But it is they who are best positioned to paint panoramic pictures of historians' practices and achievements in which the 'irreducible plurality' of historiography is neatly illustrated.

The pursuit of these and similar forms of second-order knowledge is a valuable enterprise that calls for a willingness to converse intensively with concrete specimens of actual historiography. In the following subsections, some exercises in this sort of conversation will be noticeable, especially in the mini-analyses of history texts grafted onto my pleas for reformed perspectives on some theoretical issues.

5.2 Shifting Explanatory Roles

When we allow for the plurality of historical pasts, methodological pluralism is an obvious consequence. Another, less self-evident outcome, is a more discriminating view of a pivotal question in English-speaking philosophy of history from the

1940s to the 1970s: the nature of historical explanation. The stances that were taken in this debate encompassed attempts to apply to historiography the principle that general laws and deductive inferences are constitutive elements of all truly scientific explanations; the postulate that laws and deductions are of lesser importance in the social domain as this is actually distinguished by non-natural, intentional causation; and the thesis that histories explain by telling stories articulating non-nomological and more-than-intentional causal connections between events that took place at different points in time.[134] Despite these and other major differences in the characterization of historians' explanations, most interventions in this debate since Carl Hempel's famous essay on 'The Function of General Laws in History',[135] have proceeded on the assumption that historians explain (or fail to explain) events by pointing to former occurrences and displaying them as items in a causal chain or constellation.

The preceding overview of historiography's metaphysical diversity can help us see why this basic assumption must be complexified. There is no doubt that we will find plenty of events in almost any history text we choose to read, and that historians often explain an event by reporting on former occurrences leading to it. In the perceptions of the general public, of members of neighbouring academic fields, and also in the self-images of many historians, history basically means successions of events in time and (narrative) accounts about these successions. But not all histories explain events, and not all histories explain *with* events. It is therefore necessary to extend our view to other elements that may be relevant in the economy of historical explanation.

As already stressed, entities such as persons and social individuals are sometimes prominent in historical texts; but let us concentrate on structures and discuss two different roles they can play. First, histories attentive to structures of different shapes many times aim at explaining a focus event deemed as particularly important. When they do so, they keep being histories of events, at least on their most evident content level. Decisive here, nonetheless, is that events are explained while non-events, non-observable structural factors, feature as means of explanation. Many structural histories are actually histories of events in which structures serve as key explanatory factors. In these histories, to evoke the categorial pair that is key in Hempel's deductive-nomological model, an event is the *explanandum* (that which is explained) whereas a structure – or a set of structures – plays the role of a key *explanans* (that which explains).

Consider for instance Marx's *The Eighteenth Brumaire of Louis Bonaparte*. Thematically, it is a text about political events, and, in this sense, it was, as

---

[134] See Carr, 'Narrative Explanation and Its Malcontents'; Ohara, *The Theory and Philosophy of History*, 5–10; Rüsen, *Rekonstruktion der Vergangenheit*, 22–47.

[135] Hempel, 'The Function of General Laws in History'.

Koselleck observed, a complement to the form of political history epitomized by Ranke rather than its refutation.[136] Marx proposed to explain the coup d'état whereby Louis Napoleon closed the French National Assembly in December 1851 and centralized state powers in his hands in open violation of the Constitution of the newly founded Second Republic. Marx was writing in the immediate aftermath of this focus event, hence from the position of a contemporary witness that is inescapably different from that of a historian writing in hindsight. His analysis goes back some years in time to show how the popular revolution of 1848 gave way to the authoritarian domination of Louis Napoleon. Accordingly, plenty of events preceding the 1851 coup are mentioned in the work. But Marx decisively goes beyond the task of recollecting or narratively correlating these events. Following his general view that social life and historical processes reflect the state of the material conditions in a given time and place, he directs his attention to patterns of interaction related to economic relations and social stratification, which he takes as the deep causes of the political action under explanation. As he puts it, he intended to 'demonstrate how the *class struggle* in France created circumstances and relationships that made it possible for a grotesque mediocrity [i.e. Louis Napoleon] to play a hero's part'.[137]

We stumble here on a good illustration of some of the complexities involved in historical explanations. In terms of its primary content, Marx's account is directed at the traditional domain of political action. Methodologically, however, the explanatory weight given to structural factors such as social class and productive forces moved him away from the forms that characterize conventional histories of events. Many other examples of structural histories of events could be added, and they need not be limited to the kind of conditions related to the distribution of material resources in a society as privileged by Marx, Marxists, or other schools of economic history. What I have been calling symbolic webs, that is, cultural structures, can also be endowed with explanatory powers and frequently emerge as a means of explaining individual and collective actions. In other words, they too can be elaborated into historiographical *explanantia*.[138]

There is, however, another possibility for formatting structural histories. Here, an event (or a sequence of occurrences) is no longer at the centre of a historian's explanation, but a setting itself (or a constellation of structures). Configurations of a somehow general and iterative sort, which cannot be defined in terms of events, are then pushed to the thematic forestage of historical

---

[136] Koselleck, *Begriffsgeschichten*, 54.   [137] Marx, *The Eighteenth Brumaire*, 8.
[138] Førland, *Values, Objectivity, and Explanation*, 140–5.

understanding. Different from the case exemplified with Marx's text, the focused structural configuration in this case does not play the role of a historical *explanans*, for it became itself the *explanandum*. It is no longer a means to the explanation of an event or set of events, but rather the end of the entire cognitive undertaking. Well-known classics of modern historical thought, from Voltaire's *The Age of Louis XIV* to Burckhardt's *The Civilization of the Renaissance in Italy* or Huizinga's *Autumn of the Middle Ages*, can easily be claimed as predecessors of such primary attention to structures. Indeed, serious doubts can be raised about the high grade of holism inherent in such texts.[139] But there is no doubt that in histories like these, the main *explananda* are not events, and that events play a role in them that is very different from the one they usually play in narratives that are more in line with mainstream historiographical tradition.

A compelling example is Bloch's magnum opus *Feudal Society*, which, in the author's own words, was designed to 'analyse and explain a social structure and its unifying principles'.[140] While the book presents numerous occurrences and processes, its main purpose is not to understand the causes or effects of a particular focal event. Rather, it is to illuminate a societal totality, a whole social system, one that, so to say, framed an infinity of events over a great stretch of time. Contemporary reviewers, including Bloch's close colleague Lucien Febvre, criticized the analysis for what they saw as its excessive collectivism, that is, neglect of persons and individual agency.[141] But this objection should not keep us from seeing that in Bloch's text the social structure synthesized under the term 'feudalism' is taken not as a means to the explanation of events or processes, but rather as the primary subject to be explained. His was essentially the history of a very large setting, not of particular actions or changes.

Such an analytical architecture is found also in historical works more drawn to political subjects. Richard Evans' trilogy on the Third Reich illustrates the way a complex and impactful political phenomenon may capture different kinds of historiographical attention, and that by the very same historian. In the main, Evans' text reads as a narrative, mostly structured in chronological order, of the rise and fall of the Nazi regime, that is, of transformations in what can be counted as a social individual. Volume 3, *The Third Reich at War*, almost resembles a classical history of events that can be placed in the realm of foreign politics, whereas Volume 1, *The Coming of the Third Reich*, is also mostly a history of events, but set in the framework of domestic affairs. However, in

---

[139] Gombrich, *In Search of Cultural History*.   [140] Bloch, *Feudal Society*, xvii.
[141] Rocha, *Os periódicos*, 195–7.

Volume 2, *The Third Reich in Power*, events are not the dominant *explananda*. Here, Evans is especially interested in describing social patterns that enabled and constrained the actions of people living under the Nazi regime. We could say that in this intermediary volume he delivers a mosaic-like characterization of the Third Reich as a social system, in which some sense of social totality gradually builds out of the analytic juxtaposition of views on different subsystems: the machineries of political repression and propaganda; education; welfare and judicial systems; patterns of cultural, religious, and economic life; and more.

Evans warns his readers that 'the Third Reich was not a static or monolithic dictatorship', and hence his structural depictions are far from being purely synchronic – as he mentions, they are articulated by a 'narrative thread'.[142] His analysis is very sensitive to the fact that, between 1933 and 1939, the Nazis destroyed, captured, or adapted former institutions and other structures, in addition to building new ones. Indeed, *The Third Reich in Power* addresses plenty of events and changes, conveying a complex story of Germany's preparation for war; yet its close attention to social and cultural settings stands out in comparison to the other two volumes of the project, as well as to the history-of-events tradition.

Similar negotiations characterize Bloch's *Feudal Society*. Many of its sections deal with temporally dynamic, event-like issues: the German, Muslim, and Hungarian invasions in Europe, the late-medieval 'intellectual renaissance', and the 'transformation of the nobility into a legal class', among many others. These are either structural changes or smaller-scale events that destabilized the social environment highlighted in the analysis. But they only become analytically relevant because they are seen as originating discontinuities in durations captured by structural notions such as 'mental climate', 'modes of feeling and thought', 'material conditions', and so on.

In the mode exemplified by Bloch's *Feudal System* or Evans' *The Third Reich in Power*, structural explanation means explanation *of* structures instead of explanation *by* structures. In both cases, however, it is striking how causality plays a smaller role, if any at all, than in the traditional explanation of events by events. This raises the question as to whether all relevant explanatory modes in historiography concern causality. The answer, according to Tor Egil Førland, is 'no', since historical explanations can also refer non-causally to structures or functional relations, in addition to focusing on intentional, probable, or determinant causes. In Førland's view, both structural and functional explanations can generate non-causal, yet relevant 'explanatory information' regarding

---

[142] Evans, *The Third Reich in Power*, xv–xvi.

a subject.[143] Above and beyond, when structural configurations are posed as *explanantia*, an excessive focus on issues of causation may even come to be mischievous. Overly coarse-grained attempts to show how actions, thoughts, institutions, or practices were constrained by economic or cultural structures may trigger justifiable accusations of determinism, which in historiography almost always counts as a terrible vice.

In the 1970s and 1980s, new cultural historians were particularly attentive to this risk, as they broadly endorsed Geertz's view that culture is not a causally charged 'power', but rather a 'context' within which 'social events, behaviours, institutions, or processes' 'can be intelligibly – that is, thickly – described'.[144] They sensed that cultural explanations should deliberately avoid taking symbolic structures as causal triggers of action, but nevertheless continued to see events as parts in larger wholes, which in turn appeared to them as integral factors in what happened and in its *ex post* intelligibility. Meanwhile, this has become an established and fruitful route to historical knowledge, which cannot be ignored even outside the more immediate realms of cultural history. Subtle forms of addressing cultural, social, economic, or political systems have gained a foothold, supporting non-deterministic understandings of how structural wholes weigh into events. Today, more and more historians avoid seeing structures as the immediate causes of events. They now consider that, as Sally Haslanger points out, 'social constraints set limits ..., create a choice architecture ..., structure the possibility space for agency'.[145] This entails a clear rejection of historical determinism, not necessarily of causality, but perhaps also of causalism, that is, the stance according to which only causal explanations are legitimate accounts of past and present realities.

5.3 Extensions and Limits of Exemplification

Singular, short-term events are frequently in the historiographical limelight because they matter; because some of them were particularly full of effects or are regarded as significant by the living persons and communities who generate and receive historical interpretations. The traditional interest in how an event was causally triggered, in eventful chains that can be depicted as leading to it, need not be excused. Quite the contrary, it feeds into cultural and political needs that cannot be disconnected from historiography's legitimate functions. Moreover, since the effects of 'historic' events sometimes vanish, and as they are re-signified or have their meanings altered, mnemohistorical approaches

---

[143] Førland, *Values, Objectivity, and Explanation*, 113–27.

[144] Geertz, *The Interpretation of Cultures*, 14. See also Weinstein, 'History without a Cause?', 72–8.

[145] Haslanger, 'What Is a (Social) Structural Explanation?', 117–18, 127–8.

merit a special place in the historiographical landscape. As mentioned, these approaches disclose key temporally extended dimensions attached to particularly significant occurrences, standing for an entirely renewed way of carrying out histories of events.[146]

But the role of events in historical interpretations is not restricted to that of happenings waiting to be retrospectively explained or offering themselves as reference points for prospective memory operations. As has been stressed, along with histories of events we are familiar with histories addressing conditions of possibility for acting, suffering, and thinking; that is, environmental, economic, social, cultural, and ideational settings that 'frame' events. In such histories, structural settings sometimes feature as the primary issue themselves, instead of being a means to the explanation of events or of other subjects/objects. When this happens, nonetheless, references to events fulfil a wholly different function than they do in event-centred histories. Instead of structures being summoned to help contextualize events, the latter are now introduced as a means of exemplifying structural dynamics.

What is crucial here is that events show up as epistemic resources whose function is to illustrate the way structures operate or change. As Koselleck notes, events are then approached not in terms of what came before or after them, but as indexes of structural circumstances.[147] Interestingly, the universe of occurrences that can be endowed with such a function is immense – much vaster than that of 'historic' events subjectable to explanations.

A telling case is provided by Ginzburg's *The Cheese and the Worms*, a book that was often misunderstood as inspiring a fragmentation-inducing, anecdotal style of history writing. At its focus is an extraordinary character, the sixteenth-century north-Italian miller Menocchio, who was persecuted and killed by the Inquisition in 1599 and who, among other 'heretical' views, professed that the angels, God, and human beings emerged out of primordial chaos in a process resembling the way worms grow in a putrefying cheese. Ginzburg pioneeringly adapts methodological procedures usually seen in intellectual biographies of persons from cultural elites to a study of the thoughts of an individual from the popular classes. But what goes unnoticed at times is that whereas Ginzburg's account is pervaded by biographical material, it is not simply a biography. In a sense it is much more than that, for it seeks to explain issues that go way beyond Menocchio's unconventional ideas and experiences.

Microhistorical analysis, as Ginzburg and Poni once put it, is 'bifrontal', two-pronged. On the one hand, it addresses individual experiences, but on the other, it aims at 'the invisible structures within which such experiences are

---

[146] See Section 2.2.   [147] Koselleck, *Vergangene Zukunft*, 50.

articulated'.[148] Accordingly, the study of a small-scale case such as Menocchio's should be conducted also as a platform for an inquiry into macrostructures characteristic of a past social world. *The Cheese and the Worms* indeed comprises such an inquiry. Ginzburg indicates that his investigation 'ended by developing into a general hypothesis on the popular culture (more precisely, peasant culture) of preindustrial Europe'.[149] He takes Menocchio's actions, beliefs, and words as ingredients in a microcosm, the study of which serves to ground inferences regarding the much larger macrocosm of popular culture in early modern Europe.

Whether or not this is a warranted way of drawing conclusions about large-scale cultural structures is a question that encapsulates an important methodological debate: one that is only made more complex since Menocchio was far from being a typical individual of his time, place, or class.[150] But leaving aside Ginzburg's inferential leaps from the micro to the macro levels, his way of proceeding embodies what I have called histories *of* structures. Ginzburg relates to his main character in a very empathetic way, and he is keen to convey a sense of what could have been Menocchio's personal life experiences. In effect, he sees individual actions and thoughts as much more than instances in which structural factors are deterministically reproduced or reinforced. But, at the same time, he equates personal autonomy to a 'conditional liberty', stressing that this is exercised within the 'flexible and invisible cage' of a certain culture.[151] Inasmuch as his analysis turns into a characterization of such 'cages' that frame possibilities of action, Ginzburg relates to Menocchio's experiences not as ends in themselves. In his conclusions regarding early modern popular culture, these experiences are treated as a case illustrating a point that is much more general than a person's actions and thoughts.[152]

Chiel van den Akker has recently suggested that an exemplifying way of reasoning such as that discernible in Ginzburg's work actually corresponds to the gist of historical thinking. According to van den Akker, historians' reference to events is primarily a way to illustrate vistas of the past stretching far beyond individual actions, thoughts, or attitudes. Histories bring forth 'views of or theses on the past', which are given concreteness by the narrative display of examples of bygone individual action and thought. Historians scrutinize surviving material from the past in order to learn as exactly as possible about specific events. But in so doing, their final aim is not simply to make sense of

---

[148] Ginzburg & Poni, 'Il nome e il come', 188.   [149] Ginzburg, *The Cheese and the Worms*, x.

[150] Bell, 'Total History and Microhistory', 273–4.

[151] Ginzburg, *The Cheese and the Worms*, xx–xxi.

[152] In *Proposições*, 81–3, Revel comes to similar conclusions as regards key works by Duby, Le Roy Ladurie, Davis, and Darnton.

such experiences in the same way as those who lived in the past at issue might
have done. For van den Akker, in the retrospective gaze of historians past events
are mobilized as examples in support of views of the past that must be fundamentally different from every possible view available to the contemporaries.[153]

Now is the time to point out that, like van den Akker's, some of the more
sophisticated discussions concerning what it is that histories are about do not
centre simply around the flexible notion of events, but rather around a related
one: that of change. For Peter Munz, history is not simply the study of the past,
but 'the science of change, concerned with the succession of events', and as
a result 'narrative history is history par excellence'.[154] Danto had previously
noted that in history 'the explanandum describes not simply an event – something that happens – but a change'.[155] According to him, the role of narrative in
historical knowledge is to explain changes, especially large-scale changes
unfolding over an extended period of time, on a social individual.[156] Building
upon such foundations laid by Danto, van den Akker states that 'social changes
are the primary concern of historians, and a social change is illustrated by the
behaviour of individual human beings'.[157] 'Historical narrative' – so he closes
the circle – 'is the result of the historian's retrospective understanding of social
change'.[158]

Among other things, van den Akker's perceptive analysis serves as
a reminder that there can be more at stake at the content level of histories than
events and their interconnections. But like Danto and Munz before him, van den
Akker tends to adopt a unilateral focus on social changes and events related to
them. In other words, he locates in change and in the depiction of change
(i.e. narrative) the quintessence of the 'historical'. I think this orientation is
hardly compatible with the plurality of pasts and of ways of addressing them,
which can be perceived in existing historiography. It can, therefore, be criticized
for being reductive to some degree. Depiction of change over time may be what
is most specific about historical knowledge as compared to other forms of
knowledge of human affairs. And, arguably, depiction of social, cultural,
conceptual change is its most challenging task – and perhaps also its most
interesting. Furthermore, the greater part of the histories now regarded as
paradigmatic or 'classic' are indeed works in which narrative forms predominate. In sum, there is more than one good reason to pay attention to the

---

[153] van den Akker, *The Exemplifying Past*, 11–20, 99–122.
[154] Munz, *The Shapes of Time*, 22.   [155] Danto, *Narration and Knowledge*, 233.
[156] Ibid., 255.
[157] van den Akker, *The Exemplifying Past*, 108. For an intersecting view also inspired by Danto, see
Rüsen, *Rekonstruktion der Vergangenheit*, 43–4.
[158] van den Akker, *The Exemplifying Past*, 61. Significantly, he does not speak much about
'explaining events', in causal or in other terms.

relationship between changing subjects/objects and events, and to stress that this relationship is optimally addressable by means of narrative forms of presentation. However, it may be an overgeneralization to associate the essence of history and historiography with only social or structural change. Sometimes, as in Ginzburg's *The Cheese and the Worms* or Bloch's *Feudal Society*, what is primarily at issue are not changes but structural continuities. These and other similar books by historians keep deserving to be called historical even when they characterize somehow enduring structures rather than interpret changes that unfold over time.

That said, van den Akker's insights into the exemplifying relationship between events and histories can easily be adapted to the analysis of synchronic theses such as Bloch's or Ginzburg's. The same way a historian resorts to events to illustrate a thesis regarding a social change, they can do this as a means to exemplify a view of how a structural setting functioned at a certain time. In other words, apart from exemplifying structural transformations, events can also be used to illustrate structural durations. The logic of exemplification advanced by van den Akker applies to histories dealing with both the statics and the dynamics of socio-cultural patterns.

But, and this is also important, van den Akker's analysis does not accommodate well the kind of intrinsic interest on singular occurrences that is so typical of histories of events. There are many histories that are about smaller-scale changes rather than about whatever can be conceived as a social change. More essentially – as already discussed – events, persons, texts, or artworks can attract historians' attention because they are perceived as significant singular happenings or existents by their contemporaries or by later interpreters.[159] They can be, and frequently are, addressed in contexts in which they are not bestowing concreteness upon theses concerning social wholes or structural changes. In all cultures, countless singular events are acknowledged as significant occurrences before and beyond their being referred to by one or another academic historian. Their significance is not exclusively dependent on the function they play in the framework of a single historical interpretation: it stems, to a large extent, from intertextual and extratextual social meanings that are previous to each historiographical endeavour. These tend to be the events that beg for more individualizing and less contextualist approaches; for explanations of how they came to pass, or mnemohistorical interpretations of what they came to mean after they passed. To do justice to the diversity of academic historiography, we need to find theoretical space for such histories of events. The same applies to non-narrative forms of presentation, as we shall see.

---

[159] See Sections 2.2 and 4.2.

5.4 Mixed Forms of Presentation

In its many variations, narrativism has been the dominant model for the study of historiography for the last fifty years or so. Narrativism, of course, brings to the fore the centrality of the narrative form in historical thinking. Generally speaking, it considers the basic content unit of historiography to be the event, understood in terms of individual actions functioning as vectors of surprises, novelties, and transformations. Narrativist theorists proceed on the assumption that history is fundamentally about change over time, and that to deal cognitively with change we have to narrate events; to arrange them in light of connections displayable in the form of a story. In short, once history is taken as an event-based knowledge of change, it turns out that it cannot escape from being a narrative enterprise.[160]

The association between history, change, events, and narrative has held as common sense for a long time, and it would be ludicrous to argue that such interdependences are implausible or unimportant. But I suspect that there is indeed something wrong with a stance that usually comes together with narrativism. In his thorough attempt to promote a sort of Hegelian *Aufhebung* that somehow simultaneously overcomes and continues the narrativist tradition, Jouni-Matti Kuukkanen called this problematic stance 'narrative essentialism'.[161] In my rendering, such essentialism corresponds to the sense that narrativity is a necessary condition for historicity; or, in other words, that no text or speech is historical without being organized (explicitly, covertly, or unconsciously) in the form of a narrative of events. The young Benedetto Croce expressed this view very emphatically when he stated that 'history has only one purpose: to tell facts ... History narrates'.[162]

Narrativism comprises a wide array of theoretical viewpoints, models, concepts, and insights that have decisively enriched our understanding of history writing.[163] What is more, there is yet much to be learned by historians and historical theorists from the general science of narratives developed by scholars of linguistics and literature under the name of narratology.[164] But narrative essentialism conflicts with historians' practice insofar as it takes it that, by definition, histories are or should be concerned with something that can only be depicted narratively; that is, unique, surprising, and transformative successions of events. On this assumption, non-events, existents of different sorts, are easily made light of, as well as non-narrative forms of presentation that are often manifest in historiography.

---

[160] Munz, *The Shapes of Time*, 22–5; Ricoeur, *Time and Narrative*, I, 52–94; Rüsen, *Historik*, 42–8, 75–7, 191–8; White, *The Content of the Form*, 1–25.

[161] Kuukkanen, *Postnarrativist Philosophy of Historiography*, 72–6.

[162] Croce, 'La storia ridotta', 131.   [163] Tozzi Thompson, 'Narrativism'.

[164] Kansteiner, ‚Argumentation, Beschreibung und Erzählung', 151–4.

Description, and especially what we could call 'systematic description' is a good case in point.[165] As has been stressed, historians often depict past settings and characters, taking them as stable, though not unchangeable, systems of interrelated parts.[166] In many histories, or in many passages within single history texts, focus is laid not on transformations or processes unfolding in time but on spatializable states of affairs, objects, or groups as existing at a certain temporal unit. In practice, the boundaries between narration and description can be fluid, prompting some authors to see the difference as internal to narrative discourse, which would then comprise both diachronic and synchronic stories.[167] Yet in some of these elaborations, 'narrative' is overinflated to a point where it risks becoming a category as generic as, for instance, 'interpretation' or even 'thought'. This makes it hard to imagine what would not be a narrative, not only in historiography but also in many other social sciences. From the perspective developed here, it makes greater sense to say that events are narrated dynamically, while existents can be described in their statics.[168] Examples of the latter are possibility histories shaped in a strongly synchronic way bearing essential resemblances to what Geertz called 'thick description' – an expression that aptly designates the combination of a methodological stance with a form of presentation. Influential cultural historians, and not only from recent decades, could be presented primarily as thick describers of past symbolic universes, and some of them have consciously styled themselves as such.[169]

Structural histories, in fact, may also choose to focus on economic, institutional, cultural, or conceptual changes, in which case systematic or thick description is evidently not enough. But here, too, description is heavily implied, for it would be impossible to understand the transformation of a social setting without knowing how it was configured before and after being transformed.[170] Moreover, it is important to bear in mind that structures are not simply the venues where socially predetermined scripts are enacted; that is, they are not unilateral apparatuses of social reproduction. There is indeed no unstructured event, no human action or suffering disconnected from already existing structural conditions of possibility. Even so, every event is unique, and some of

---

[165] Criticizing Saussure's structural view of linguistics, Coseriu, *Sincronía, diacronía e historia*, 23, plays 'history' against 'systematic description'. I borrow this last term from him, even though my argument runs counter to the rigid opposition originally denoted by it.

[166] Prost, *Douze leçons*, ch. 9.   [167] White, *Metahistory*, 10–11.

[168] Koselleck, *Vergangene Zukunft*, 144–52. As will be mentioned, changes in existents are also narratable. It should be noted that I am relying here on a distinction between narrative and non-narrative forms of presentation that is not undisputed among narratologists. See Ryan, 'Toward a Definition of Narrative', 26–8.

[169] Geertz, *The Interpretation of Cultures*, 1–30; Clark, *History, Theory, Text*, 145–55.

[170] Sewell, *Logics of History*, 184–5.

them are seen as surprising, path-breaking, radically new occurrences affecting the functioning of structures, promoting their change. Sewell connects this potentiality to the fact that the persons involved in events always live within the range of different structures. On his account, collective creativity is not tied to anomalies or individual congeniality, but is itself backed by structural reasons. It results from the translation and application of codes, rules, and categories from one structural domain to another.[171]

Structural changes and large-scale processes are a key topic I will not be able to discuss at length. The presentations of what Pierre Villar called 'de-structurations' and 're-structurations' involve metaphysical ingredients lacking in traditional presentations of sequences of events witnessed by their contemporaries.[172] It is fair to say, however, that in both cases historical texts take a predominantly narrative shape, because, again, narrative is our standard cognitive device for dealing with change unfolding in time. Moreover, since events are downwardly divisible and upwardly aggregable, there is no logical obstacle to equating a slow-motion social process to an event. But in practice such a complex sort of event would firmly resist being bracketed together with the kind of individual action usually taken as paradigmatic in narrative analyses. How narrative form is affected by the visibility, scale, and tempo of the primary changes it thematizes is a question that deserves more attention from theorists of historical representation than it has received.

As is evident, while dissociating my tentative view of these issues from the stance introduced as 'narrative essentialism', I recognize that narrative has a very broad presence in the historiographical domain. Even so, it is important to underline that historians do more than narrate bygone events. And, for that matter, they also do more than describe past characters and settings. At least in academic historiography, texts are constituted not just by statements referring to what was or what happened in the past, but also by passages that foreground logical rather than temporal relations between abstract subjects/objects,[173] in which reasons are provided for accepting or rejecting narrations and descriptions. This is why we should add argumentation to the mix of the forms of presentation usually prominent in histories. Calling attention to history writing as an argumentative practice, Kuukkanen has even claimed that narrative passages in historical texts are actually subsidiary to their more general argumentative components. Historians, he claims, not only deliver comprehensive theses about the past, but also articulate and display evidence in support of those theses, with the aim of persuading the reading audience to accept them.

---

[171] Ibid., 140–3, 209–13, 250–1.   [172] Quoted in Malerba, *Ensaios*, 106.
[173] See Aumüller, 'Text Types', 854.

This would be the most fundamental operation in historiography, and it may involve narrativization in more than one way; but crucially, it need not. According to Kuukkanen, one of the argumentative, evidence-based means of securing 'epistemic authority' to historiographical theses is, by the way, to exemplify them by referring to singular courses of action.[174]

At the very least, then, we have *argumentations*, *descriptions* of characters and settings of varying types and magnitudes, in addition to *narrations* of either smaller-scale events that were visible to their contemporaries or larger-scale processes that could not have been observed as such at the time they unfolded. These and other combinations of forms of presentation and content-related focal points may be found in historical texts. As a result, it becomes rather difficult to maintain that simply the narration of successive events extending over a lapse of time is by default their most essential distinguishing feature. As proposed by Wulf Kansteiner, a good way to make sense of historical texts is to view them as multi-layered, hybrid products, constituted by at least narrations, descriptions, and argumentations. The balance between these three basic text types varies from case to case, most histories indeed containing robust narrative components, but never being simply devoid of descriptive or argumentative passages and sentences. Narrative depictions of change over time rely, in differing degrees and ways, on descriptions of characters and settings. Descriptions and narrations need to be backed, in turn, by evidence-related argumentative webs. Descriptive or argumentative moves can overpower and subordinate narrations in a text, causing its primary shape to be very different from that of a story. Each of the three text types can predominate and coordinate the functions played by the other two in a concrete text. But historiography as an abstract whole cannot be aprioristically reduced to any one of them.[175] This realization should encourage the development of new models of analysis that dispense with the hierarchical ordering of historiographical forms of presentation and, by implication, with the assumption that one of these forms is closer to the core of historicity than the others.

---

[174] Kuukkanen, *Postnarrativist Philosophy of Historiography*, 66–70, 83–96.

[175] Kansteiner, 'Argumentation, Beschreibung und Erzählung', 154–6; Kansteiner, 'History beyond Narration', 53–5. Regarding the narratological discussion on which Kansteiner draws here, see Aumüller, 'Text Types'.

Coda

An old methodological habit prescribes that history is inherently attached to a diachronic perspective, whereas most other social sciences are synchronically oriented. History, on this account, traces the development of events and states of affairs in time, possibly up to the present, while the social sciences have a special licence to suspend time analytically and focus on spatializable patterns characteristic of contemporary societies.

It would be convenient were such a nice and clear division of labour justifiable, but it is not. It is undermined by the existence of approaches very much centred on change within, for instance, anthropology, political science, or law; or of historical sociology – a branch of the social sciences which is as old as sociology itself. Moreover, it neglects the fact that there is actually a third way beyond the characterization of the social world in terms of its contemporary structural configurations and the depiction of temporal changes in structures, social individuals, ideas, or persons. Not only structural configurations of the present, but also those of the past can be at the centre of social analyses. In fact, many scholars dealing with pasts are less concerned with changes and events than with permanencies in settings and characters. To name inquiries and texts that focus more on past durations than changes, more on what *was* than on what *happened*, we have no other word but 'history'.

We stumble here over two distinct, sometimes competing, key meanings of terms such as 'history', 'historical', and 'historicising'. For these words point not only to change, to transformations that were full of consequences or are regarded as particularly significant. When we say 'historical', we sometimes mean simply something or some event 'in the past' that no longer belongs to our contemporary world. History hence encompasses both a sense of temporal change and a sense of the pastness of the past; it can indicate either temporal movement, or temporal containment, or both simultaneously.[176] The first sense underpins a genetic approach centred on events succeeding one another in time, events that caused (or can be worked out to illustrate) changes taking place on existents. Narrative is its associated form of presentation. The other sense serves as the basis for a systemic approach that privileges spatial contiguity and directs attention to enduring regularities as existing at a certain, analytically frozen, moment in time. This approach feeds into cross-sectional, structural descriptions. As the late Peter Reill pointed out, both analytical strategies have

---

[176] Gordon, 'Contextualism and Criticism', 34–5; Sewell, *Logics of History*, 182–3.

cohabited in a complementary and occasionally tense relation since at least the late eighteenth century. Commenting on German historians from the time of the late Enlightenment, Reill argued that 'although theoretically complementary, the two strategies of structural and developmental analysis forced the researcher to adopt contradictory tactics of investigation and modes of representation . . . . The tension between these two interests forms one of the constants in the modern discussion of the form and nature of historical inquiry.'[177]

Most of this Element was an attempt to factor in and account for the tension Reill so aptly spotted. I started from the intuition that sometimes histories are mainly about contents that cannot be categorized as unique events. Now, I am ending with the suggestion that together with the idea that history is essentially about events we should also consider giving up the idea that it is essentially narrative. My call for a heightened sensitivity to the plurality of historical pasts has turned out to be a possible metaphysical complement to non-narrativist theses such as those recently advanced by Kansteiner and Kuukkanen from narratological and epistemological points of view. In any case, the reasons we have for moving beyond an event-centric understanding of historical know-ledge seem to be closely related to those prompting us to pay more attention to non-narrative modes of presentation identifiable in it, such as description and argumentation. Whenever those reasons are neglected, we risk arriving at a picture of historiography that generalizes too much from only one of the two basic meanings of 'historicizing'. As I have been proposing, such a reduction of complexity vis-à-vis the historical can, and should, be avoided.

---

[177] Reill, *The German Enlightenment and the Rise of Historicism*, 38–40.

References

Ankersmit, Frank, *Meaning, Truth, and Reference in Historical Representation.* Ithaca, NY: Cornell University Press, 2012.

Araújo, André de Melo, 'Imagens da simultaneidade e os impasses da narrativa: O caso da "Synopsis historiae universalis" (1766) de Johann Christoph Gatterer', *Tempo* 21 (2015), 192–215.

Aristotle, *Posterior Analytics.* Oxford: Blackwell, 1901.

Aristotle, *Poetics.* Indianapolis, IN: Hackett, 1987.

Assmann, Jan, *Moses the Egyptian: The Memory of Egypt in Western Monotheism.* Cambridge, MA: Harvard University Press, 1997.

Aumüller, Matthias, 'Text Types', in Peter Hühn, John Pier, Wolf Schmid, & Jörg Schönert (eds.), *Handbook of Narratology, Volume 2.* Berlin: De Gruyter, 2014, 854–67.

Bachmann-Medick, Doris, *Cultural Turns: Neuorientierungen in den Kulturwissenschaften.* Hamburg: Reinbek, 2006.

Balmaceda, Catalina, 'La Antigüedad clásica: Grecia y Roma', in Jaume Aurell, Catalina Balmaceda, Peter Burke, & Felipe Soza (eds.), *Comprender el passado. Una historia de Ia escritura y el pensamiento histórico.* Madrid: Akal, 2013, 9–58.

Bell, David A., 'Total History and Microhistory', in Lloyd Kramer & Sarah Maza (eds.), *A Companion to Western Historical Thought.* Malden, MA: Blackwell, 2006, 262–76.

Bloch, Marc, *The Historian's Craft.* New York: Vintage, 1953.

Bloch, Marc, *Feudal Society.* London: Routledge, 2014.

Bösch, Frank, 'Das historische Ereignis', in *Dokupedia-Zeitgeschichte.* Potsdam: Zentrum für Zeithistorische Forschung, 2020. http://dx.doi.org/10.14765/zzf.dok-1754.

Braudel, Fernand, *On History.* Chicago, IL: The University of Chicago Press, 1980.

Braudel, Fernand, *The Mediterranean and the Mediterranean World in the Age of Philip II*, 2 vols. Berkeley: University of California Press, 1995.

Capdevila, Luc, *Paraguay bajo la sombra de sus guerras: Historia, memoria y construcción política, siglos XIX/XXI.* Madrid: Sb, 2021.

Carr, David, 'Narrative Explanation and Its Malcontents', *History and Theory* 47 (2008), 19–30.

Casati, Roberto & Varzi, Achille, 'Events', in *Stanford Encyclopedia of Philosophy*, 2020. https://plato.stanford.edu/archives/sum2020/entries/events/.

Cassirer, Ernst, *The Philosophy of Symbolic Forms, Volume 1: Language*. London: Routledge, 2021.

Chatman, Seymour, *Story and Discourse: Narrative Structure in Fiction and Film*. Ithaca, NY: Cornell University Press, 1978.

Chazel, François, 'Social Structure', in P. Baltes & N. Smelser (eds.), *International Encyclopedia of the Social & Behavioral Sciences*. Amsterdam: Elsevier, 2001, 15233–7.

Cheng, Eileen Ka-May, *Historiography: An Introductory Guide*. London: Continuum, 2012.

Christian, David, *Maps of Time: An Introduction to Big History*. Berkeley: University of California Press, 2004.

Clark, Elizabeth A., *History, Theory, Text: Historians and the Linguistic Turn*. Cambridge, MA: Harvard University Press, 2004.

Coseriu, Eugenio, *Sincronía, diacronía e historia: El problema del cambio lingüístico*. Madrid: Gredos, 1978.

Croce, Benedetto, 'La storia ridotta sotto il concetto generale dell'arte', *Atti dell'Accademia pontaniana*, XXIII (1893), 118–49.

Danto, Arthur, *Narration and Knowledge*. New York: Columbia University Press, 2007.

Daston, Lorraine, 'Baconian Facts, Academic Civility, and the Prehistory of Objectivity', in Allan Megill (ed.), *Rethinking Objectivity*. Durham, NC: Duke University Press, 1994, 37–63.

Davis, Natalie Z., *The Return of Martin Guerre*. Cambridge, MA: Harvard University Press, 1983.

Doratioto, Francisco, *Maldita Guerra: Nova história da Guerra do Paraguai*. São Paulo: Companhia das Letras, 2002.

Dosse, François, *History of Structuralism, Volume 1: The Rising Sign (1945–1966)*. Minneapolis: University of Minnesota Press, 1997.

Dosse, François, 'Historical Event between the Sphinx and the Phoenix', in Marek Tamm (ed.), *Afterlife of Events: Perspectives on Mnemohistory*. Basingstoke: Palgrave Macmillan, 2015, 27–43.

Droysen, Johann G., *Historik: Vorlesungen über Enzyklopädie und Methodologie der Geschichte*. Munich: Oldenbourg, 1971.

Durkheim, Émile, *The Rules of Sociological Method and Selected Texts on Sociology and Its Method*. Basingstoke: Palgrave Macmillan, 2013.

Elder-Vass, Dave, 'Material Parts in Social Structures', *Journal of Social Ontology* 3 (2017), 89–105.

Epstein, Brian, *The Ant Trap: Rebuilding the Foundations of the Social Sciences*. Oxford: Oxford University Press, 2015.

Epstein, Brian, 'Social Ontology', in *Stanford Encyclopedia of Philosophy*, 2018. https://plato.stanford.edu/entries/social-ontology/.

Evans, Richard, *The Coming of the Third Reich*. New York: Penguin, 2004.

Evans, Richard, *The Third Reich in Power*. London: Penguin, 2006.

Fillion, Real, 'The Continuing Relevance of Speculative Philosophy of History', *Journal of the Philosophy of History* 8 (2014), 180–95.

Førland, Tor E., *Values, Objectivity, and Explanation in Historiography*. London: Routledge, 2017.

Gadamer, Hans-Georg, *Gesammelte Werke, Band I: Wahrheit und Methode*. Tübingen: Mohr, 1990.

Geertz, Clifford, *The Interpretation of Cultures: Selected Essays*. New York: Basic Books, 1973.

Giddens, Anthony, *The Constitution of Society: Outline of the Theory of Structuration*. London: Polity, 1997.

Ginzburg, Carlo, *The Cheese and the Worms: The Cosmos of a Sixteenth-Century Miller*. Baltimore, MD: The Johns Hopkins University Press, 1992.

Ginzburg, Carlo & Poni, Carlo, 'Il nome e il come: scambio ineguale e mercato storiografico', *Quaderni storici* 14 (1979), 181–90.

Goethe, Johann Wolfgang, *Zur Farbenlehre*, Band II. Tübingen: J.-G. Cotta'sche Buchhandlung, 1810.

Gombrich, Ernst H., *In Search of Cultural History*. Oxford: Clarendon, 1969.

Gordon, Peter E., 'Contextualism and Criticism in the History of Ideas', in Samuel Moyn & Darrin McMahon (eds.), *Modern Intellectual History: Reappraisals and New Perspectives for the Twenty-First Century*. Oxford: Oxford University Press, 2013, 32–55.

Hacking, Ian, *Historical Ontology*. Cambridge, MA: Harvard University Press, 2002.

Haslanger, Sally, 'What Is a (Social) Structural Explanation?', *Philosophical Studies* 173 (2016), 113–30.

Hempel, Carl G., 'The Function of General Laws in History', *Journal of Philosophy* 39 (1942), 35–48.

Herculano, Alexandre, *Opúsculos, Volume VI*. Lisbon: Bertrand, n.d.

Herodotus, *The Histories*. Oxford: Oxford University Press, 2008.

Hobsbawm, Eric, *Age of Extremes: The Short Twentieth Century, 1914–1991*. London: Abacus, 1995.

Hughes-Warrington, Marnie, *Big and Little Histories: Sizing Up Ethics in Historiography*. London: Routledge, 2021.

Huizinga, Johan, *The Autumn of the Middle Ages*. Chicago, IL: Chicago University Press, 1996.

Humboldt, Wilhelm von, 'On the Historian's Task', *History and Theory* 6 (1967), 57–71.

Iggers, Georg G. & Wang, Q. Edward, *A Global History of Modern Historiography*. Harlow: Pearson Longman, 2008.

Jay, Martin, 'Historical Explanation and the Event: Reflections on the Limits of Contextualization', *New Literary History* 42 (2011), 557–71.

Jung, Theo & Karla, Anna, 'Times of the Event: An Introduction', *History and Theory* 60 (2021), 75–85.

Kansteiner, Wulf, 'Argumentation, Beschreibung und Erzählung in der wissenschaftlichen Historiographie', in Thomas Sandkühler & Horst Walter Blanke (eds.), *Historisierung der Historik: Jörn Rüsen zum 80. Geburtstag*. Köln: Böhlau, 2018, 151–68.

Kansteiner, Wulf, 'History beyond Narration: The Shifting Terrain of Bloodlands', in Stefan Berger, Nicola Brauch, & Chris Lorenz (eds.), *Analysing Historical Narratives: On Academic, Popular and Educational Framings of the Past*. New York: Berghahn, 2021, 51–82.

Karla, Anna, 'Controversial Chronologies: The Temporal Demarcation of Historic Events', *History and Theory* 60 (2021), 134–49.

Kleinberg, Ethan, *Haunting History: For a Deconstructive Approach to the Past*. Stanford, CA: Stanford University Press, 2017.

Kocka, Jürgen, *Sozialgeschichte: Begriff – Entwicklung – Probleme*. Göttingen: Vandenhoeck & Ruprecht, 1986.

Koselleck, Reinhart, *Vergangene Zukunft: Zur Semantik geschichtlicher Zeiten*. Frankfurt: Suhrkamp, 1989.

Koselleck, Reinhart, *Zeitschichten: Studien zur Historik*. Frankfurt: Suhrkamp, 2003.

Koselleck, Reinhart, *Begriffsgeschichten: Studien zur Semantik und Pragmatik der politischen und sozialen Sprache*. Frankfurt: Suhrkamp, 2010.

Koselleck, Reinhart, *Vom Sinn und Unsinn der Geschichte*. Frankfurt: Suhrkamp, 2010.

Kuukkanen, Jouni-Matti, *Postnarrativist Philosophy of Historiography*. Basingstoke: Palgrave Macmillan, 2015.

Kuukkanen, Jouni-Matti, 'Fact', in Stefan Berger (ed.), *Bloomsbury History: Theory and Method*. London: Bloomsbury, 2021. http://dx.doi.org/10.5040/9781350970885.072.

Little, Daniel, *New Contributions to the Philosophy of* History. Dordrecht: Springer, 2010.

Mahdi, Muhsin, *Ibn Khaldûn's Philosophy of History: A Study in the Philosophic Foundation of the Science of Culture*. London: Routledge, 2016.

Malerba, Jurandir, *Ensaios: teoria, história e ciências sociais*. Londrina: Eduel, 2011.

Martin, John L., *Social Structures*. Princeton, NJ: Princeton University Press, 2009.

Marx, Karl, *The Eighteenth Brumaire of Louis Bonaparte*. New York: International Publishers, 1963.

Marx, Karl, *A Contribution to the Critique of Political Economy*. Moscow: Progress Publishers, 1977.

Mauldin, Erin Stewart, 'Environmental History', in Stefan Berger (ed.), *Bloomsbury History: Theory and Method*. London: Bloomsbury, 2021. http://dx.doi.org/10.5040/9781350970847.043.

McCullagh, C. Behan, *The Truth of* History. London: Routledge, 1998.

Megill, Allan, *Historical Knowledge, Historical Error: A Contemporary Guide to Practice*. Chicago, IL: Chicago University Press, 2007.

Mergel, Thomas, 'Kulturgeschichte der Politik', in Frank Bösch & Jürgen Danyel (eds.), *Zeitgeschichte: Konzepte und Methoden*. Göttingen: Vandenhoeck & Ruprecht, 2012, 187–203.

Mink, Louis O., *Historical Understanding*. Ithaca, NY: Cornell University Press, 1987.

Munz, Peter, *The Shapes of Time: A New Look at the Philosophy of History*. Middletown, NY: Wesleyan University Press, 1977.

Offenburger, Andrew, 'The Xhosa Cattle-Killing Movement in History and Literature', *History Compass*, 7 (2009), 1428–43.

Ohara, João, *The Theory and Philosophy of History: Global Variations*. Cambridge: Cambridge University Press, 2022.

Pedersen, Susan, 'What Is Political History Now?', in David Cannadine (ed.), *What Is History Now?* Basingstoke: Palgrave Macmillan, 2002, 36–56.

Peires, Jeffrey B., *The Dead Will Arise: Nongqawuse and the Great Xhosa Cattle-Killing Movement of 1856–7*. Johannesburg: Raven Press, 1989.

Pereira, Mateus H. F., 'A história entre os inimigos do evento e os advogados da estrutura', *Ler História* 57 (2009), 59–71.

Peters, Gabriel, *Percursos na teoria das práticas sociais: Anthony Giddens e Pierre Bourdieu*. São Paulo: Annablume, 2015.

Phillips, Mark S., *Society and Sentiment: Genres of Historical Writing in Britain, 1740–1820*. Princeton, NJ: Princeton University Press, 2000.

Polybius, *The Histories, Volume I*. Cambridge, MA: Harvard University Press, 1998.

Pomian, Krzysztof, 'Evento', in *Enciclopédia Einaudi, Volume 29*. Lisbon: INCM, 1993, 214–35.

Pomian, Krzysztof, *Sur l'histoire*. Paris: Gallimard, 1999.

Prost, Antoine, *Douze leçons sur l'histoire*. Paris: Seuil, 1996.

Raphael, Lutz, 'Die "Neue Geschichte" – Umbrüche und Neue Wege der Geschichtsschreibung in internationaler Perspektive (1880–1940)', in Wolfgang Küttler, Jörn Rüsen, & Ernst Schulin (eds.), *Geschichtsdiskurs, Volume 4*. Frankfurt: Fischer, 1997, 51–89.

Raphael, Lutz, *Geschichtswissenschaft im Zeitalter der Extreme: Theorien, Methoden, Tendenzen von 1900 bis zur Gegenwart*. Munich: Beck, 2003.

Reill, Peter H., *The German Enlightenment and the Rise of Historicism*. Berkeley: University of California Press, 1975.

Retz, Tyson, *Progress and the Scale of History*. Cambridge: Cambridge University Press, 2022.

Revel, Jacques, *Proposições: Ensaios de História e Historiografia*. Rio de Janeiro: Ed. UERJ, 2009.

Rickert, Heinrich, *The Limits of Concept Formation in Natural Science*. Cambridge: Cambridge University Press, 2009.

Ricœur, Paul, *Time and Narrative, Volume I*. Chicago, IL: Chicago University Press, 1984.

Ritchie, Katherine, 'Social Structures and the Ontology of Social Groups', *Philosophy and Phenomenological Research* 100 (2020), 402–24.

Rocha, Sabrina Magalhães, *Os periódicos e a crítica da história: A recepção de Lucien Febvre por seus contemporâneos*. Vitória: Milfontes, 2021.

Romano, Claude, *Event and World*. New York: Fordham University Press, 2009.

Roth, Paul A., *The Philosophical Structure of Historical Explanation*. Evanston, IL: Northwestern University Press, 2020.

Rüsen, Jörn, *Rekonstruktion der Vergangenheit: Grundzüge einer Historik II: Die Prinzipien der historischen Forschung*. Göttingen: Vandenhoeck & Ruprecht, 1986.

Rüsen, Jörn, *Historik: Theorie der Geschichtswissenschaft*. Cologne: Böhlau, 2013.

Ryan, Marie-Laure, 'Toward a Definition of Narrative', in David Herman (ed.), *The Cambridge Companion to Narrative*. Cambridge: Cambridge University Press, 2007, 22–35.

Scholtz, Oliver R., 'Philosophy of History: Metaphysics and Epistemology', in Marie Kaiser, Oliver R. Scholz, Daniel Plenge, & Andreas Hüttemann (eds.), *Explanation in the Special Sciences: The Cases of Biology and History*. Dordrecht: Springer, 2014, 245–53.

Serna, Justo & Pons, Anaclet, *La historia cultural: autores, obras, lugares*. Madrid: Akal, 2013.

Sewell Jr, William, *Logics of History: Social Theory and Social Transformation*. Chicago, IL: University of Chicago Press, 2005.

Simiand, François, 'Historical Method and Social Science', *Review* 9 (1985), 163–213.

Sreedharan, E., *A Textbook of Historiography, 500 BC to AD 2000*. Hyderabad: Orient BlackSwan, 2017.

Tamm, Marek, 'Introduction', in Marek Tamm (ed.), *Afterlife of Events: Perspectives on Mnemohistory*. Basingstoke: Palgrave Macmillan, 2015, 1–23.

Tozzi Thompson, Verónica, 'Narrativism', in Chiel van den Akker (ed.), *The Routledge Companion to Historical Theory*. London: Routledge, 2022, 113–28.

Tucker, Aviezer. *Our Knowledge of the Past: A Philosophy of Historiography*. Cambridge: Cambridge University Press, 2004.

van den Akker, Chiel, *The Exemplifying Past: A Philosophy of History*. Amsterdam: Amsterdam University Press, 2018.

Veyne, Paul, *Writing History: Essay on Epistemology*. Manchester: Manchester University Press, 1984.

Walbank, Frank, *Polybius*. Berkeley: University of California Press, 1990.

Weinstein, Barbara, 'History without a Cause? Grand Narratives, World History, and the Postcolonial Dilemma', *International Review of Social History* 50 (2005), 71–93.

Welskopp, Thomas, 'Die Sozialgeschichte Der Väter: Grenzen und Perspektiven der Historischen Sozialwissenschaft', *Geschichte und Gesellschaft* 24 (1998), 173–98.

White, Hayden, *Metahistory: The Historical Imagination in Nineteenth-Century Europe*. Baltimore MD: The Johns Hopkins University Press, 1973.

White, Hayden, *The Content of the Form: Narrative Discourse and Historical Representation*. Baltimore, MD: Johns Hopkins University Press, 1987.

Woolf, Daniel, *A Global History of History*. Cambridge: Cambridge University Press, 2011.

Zeleňák, Eugen, 'Two Approaches to Event Ontology', *Organon F* 3 (2009), 283–303.

Acknowledgements

The basic ideas presented in this Element were developed in or for the classroom, in the context of the many 'Introduction to the Study of History' courses I have been offering at the University of Brasilia for more than a decade. Through their questions and comments over the years, numerous students have helped to sharpen my views on the plurality of academic historiography. I am indebted to them, even to those whose faces I have never seen due to the unchosen conditions of remote online teaching during the 'pandemic' semesters between 2020 and 2022 – a period that was crucial for the elaboration of my argument.

I would like to thank all the friends and colleagues who discussed the project with me or commented on parts of the manuscript, especially members of the Permanent Forum for Historical Theory at the Federal University of Goiás and participants in the Theory of History Workshop at the University of Brasilia. I am also very grateful to Marnie Hughes-Warrington and the two anonymous reviewers for their valuable criticisms and suggestions, and to Daniel Woolf for the careful feedback provided at different stages of the project. At home, I thank Elisa and Vânia for the life that we share. Brazil's National Council for Scientific and Technological Development (CNPq) sponsored the research.

Cambridge Elements ≡

Historical Theory and Practice

Daniel Woolf
Queen's University, Ontario

Daniel Woolf is Professor of History at Queen's University, where he served for ten years as Principal and Vice-Chancellor, and has held academic appointments at a number of Canadian universities. He is the author or editor of several books and articles on the history of historical thought and writing, and on early modern British intellectual history, including most recently *A Concise History of History* (CUP 2019). He is a Fellow of the Royal Historical Society, the Royal Society of Canada, and the Society of Antiquaries of London. He is married with 3 adult children.

About the Series
Cambridge Elements in Historical Theory and Practice is a series intended for a wide range of students, scholars, and others whose interests involve engagement with the past. Topics include the theoretical, ethical, and philosophical issues involved in doing history, the interconnections between history and other disciplines and questions of method, and the application of historical knowledge to contemporary global and social issues such as climate change, reconciliation and justice, heritage, and identity politics.

Cambridge Elements ☰

Historical Theory and Practice

Elements in the Series

A History of Political Science
Mark Bevir

The Theory and Philosophy of History: Global Variations
João Ohara

The Transformation of History in the Digital Age
Ian Milligan

Historians' Virtues: From Antiquity to the Twenty-First Century
Herman Paul

Confronting Evil in History
Daniel Little

Progress and the Scale of History
Tyson Retz

*Collaborative Historical Research in the Age of Big Data: Lessons
from an Interdisciplinary Project*
Ruth Ahnert, Emma Griffin, Mia Ridge and Giorgia Tolfo

A History of Big History
Ian Hesketh

Archaeology as History: Telling Stories from a Fragmented Past
Catherine J. Frieman

The Fabric of Historical Time
Zoltán Boldizsár Simon, Marek Tamm

Writing the History of Global Slavery
Trevor Burnard

Plural Pasts: Historiography between Events and Structures
Arthur Alfaix Assis

A full series listing is available at: www.cambridge.org/EHTP

Printed in the United States
by Baker & Taylor Publisher Services